SWEDISH FOOD

New Completely Revised Edition by

Greta Borgstrom and

Birgit Danfors

WEZÄTA FÖRLAG GÖTEBORG SWEDEN

Why Swedish Food has been Revised

SWEDISH FOOD was first published in 1948. The initiative and idea
to the book came from the publisher, Mr. Sam Widenfelt, and it
was the joint work of the Home Economics Department of the
Publisher and Mrs. *Emmie Berg,* graduate of Cordon Bleu, Paris,
and former resident of Mont Clair, New Jersey. Mrs *Greta Ström-
bäck-Borgstrom,* on the Publisher's editorial staff, supervised the
making of the book.

SWEDISH FOOD became an immediate success, and over the past
fifteen years it has been printed in no less than fifteen editions,
totally amounting to 125,000 copies. A decade and a half is a
fairly lengthy life-span for a cookbook. In general it is not
appreciated how much day-to-day living changes over such a long
period. Dietary habits are also affected. New food products come
on the market, new kitchen equipment and household gadgets are
provided. The advances of the science of nutrition has in many
ways a substantial effect on our eating patterns. Through research
in the field of home economics, cooking techniques and methods
in food preparation have been improved and simplified. These are
the basic reasons for the revision undertaken with *Swedish Food.*
It has been brought up to date with regard to all these innovations.
The recipes have been kitchen-tested anew in the United States and
thoroughly adapted to present-day conditions. A reevaluation has
also been made of what constitutes the living tradition in Swedish
cooking and dietary habits, and this has dictated the new selec-
tion of recipes.

In conducting this major modernizing revision, the Publisher has

3

been fortunate to be able to rely upon the services of Mrs. Greta Borgstrom, who originally supervised the book. Since 1957 she resides in East Lansing, Michigan. She has provided new introductory texts to the various recipe sections conveying a more comprehensive picture of present-day Swedish food habits with special emphasis of how they tie in with the rich traditions of the country, those connected with its everyday life as well as with its many holidays and their colorful rituals. For the reediting and kitchen-testing of the recipes to guarantee their easy use by today's home-maker, Mrs. Borgstrom worked closely with Mrs. *Birgit Danfors*, an experienced Swedish home economist, who for some time resided in East Lansing.

In its new appearance, SWEDISH FOOD constitutes a most up to date and reliable guide to the many delights of the *Smörgåsbord* as well as to Swedish cooking traditions in general, as they prevail and are practised in the native country. For those who own a copy of the original *Swedish Food* — whether worn out or not — its replacement with this new and completely revised edition will provide additional joy and ease in practising genuine Swedish cooking and entertaining. For newcomers in the field, the *new Swedish Food* opens the door to fine new experiences in creative cooking.

Göteborg, Sweden, January, 1965
WEZÄTA FÖRLAG

Contents

Some Useful Hints

The U.S. standard kitchen cup, tablespoon (tbsp.), and teaspoon (tsp.) are the measures used in the recipes. All measures are level.

Can sizes, when given, refer to American standard sizes. The equivalent in volume or weight is stated in the recipes.

Flour used in the recipes is all-purpose flour, except when otherwise indicated.

Vinegar used in testing the recipes is regular American "Distilled White Vinegar, diluted with water to a uniform pickling and table strength of 5 % acidity". If vinegar of a higher strength of acidity is used, adjustment should be made by diluting it with water.

Cornstarch here replaces potato starch flour, commonly used in Swedish cooking. 1 tablespoon cornstarch is the equivalent of 1 tablespoon "potato flour". The latter is generally on sale in Scandinavian delicatessen shops for the convenience of those who want to use it in recipes from "the old country".

Margarine can be substituted for butter in all recipes.

Conversion Tables

To facilitate the use of the recipes in countries with a measure system different from that of the U.S. the following tables are helpful:

Conversion Table for Some Measures

1 cup = $1/2$ pint = $2^1/4$ decilitres
1 cup butter (2 American sticks) = $1/2$ pound = 225 grams
1 package dry yeast = 1 cake compressed fresh yeast = $2/3$ or $3/5$ ounce = about 20 grams
1 envelope unflavored gelatin = 1 tbsp. thickens 1 pint (2 cups) liquid. It corresponds to 4–5 Swedish gelatin leaves.

The American measuring cup is 8 fluid ounces. If the British cup of half-pint size, made a standard for kitchen measuring cups, is used, the results will be proportionally larger.

Oven Temperature Conversion Table (Rounded figures)

	°F	°C
Very slow	250–275	125–135
Slow	300–325	150–175
Moderate	350–375	175–200
Hot	400–425	200–225
Very hot	450–475	225–250
Extremely hot	500–525	250–275

Introduction

This book will take you on a cruise to the delicacies of the Swedish table, including Smörgåsbord and other famous specialties. The many pictures and the detailed, kitchen-tested recipes will enable you to rejoice in preparing them in your own kitchen. In introductory texts to each chapter, the food and eating habits of the country and the traditions behind them are put forth.

The recipes are chosen primarily with an eye to their appeal to the modern palate, but also to represent what can be termed the authentic Swedish kitchen, both modern and traditional. The recent visitor to Sweden will recognize many dishes and foods enjoyed on the spot and will be able to prepare them at home. The Swedish immigrant or descendant abroad gets the genuine descriptions for preparing many old culinary acquaintances, although adapted to today's food products and cooking techniques.

The Swedes, like any other modern nation, today practice a much more varied kitchen than a generation or two ago. Canning and freezing, refrigeration and importation have made all kinds of fruits,vegetables and other items, which cannot be produced locally owing to climatic or other reasons, easily available the year round through well-stocked food stores all over the country. Most farms and many other homes are provided with freezing units, and a refrigerator, as well as other modern devices, belonging to the standard equipment of the kitchen. All these factors have brought tremendous changes to Swedish cooking and eating habits during this century. Modern nutritional science also had a profound impact. Among what can be termed traditional dishes today, many are still as cherished and as common as in the old days. Others have lost their appeal, being too sturdy or too removed from modern taste.

Too elaborate preparation has made the Swedes discard quite a few traditional dishes no longer characteristic to the present everyday diet in this age of convenience foods. In the case of some old favorites, industry and institutions have taken over their cooking and thus saved them from vanishing. Others again have survived as special holiday treats, particularly at Christmas time.

The recipes here represent the living tradition in Swedish cooking. They offer you rewarding cooking experiences and give you the thrills of culinary adventures from Sweden — the home of the Smörgåsbord.

GRETA BORGSTROM   BIRGIT DANFORS

Some Swedish
Specialty Foods

The ingredients in the recipes of this book are available in super-markets and other well-stocked food stores in the U.S. and other Western countries. Only a few dishes call for Swedish ingredients, available outside the country, mostly in Scandinavian specialty stores. Information about these products is given immediately under the recipe head when there is only one dish in the book based upon a special ingredient. About specialty foods mentioned in more than one recipe, information is given below.

Swedish Anchovies, also marked *Marinated Sprats in Can, in lobster sauce or spiced sauce* is a piquant ingredient in many Smörgåsbord dishes. It is packed whole in 10 to 14-oz. cans containing 20 to 30 sprats, and in fillets in smaller cans containing about 3½ oz. or 15 to 20 fillets. In Sweden it is a favorite companion to the boiled breakfast eggs.

Swedish Caviar, also marked *Cod Roe Spread,* is a common, salty sandwich spread often garnished with chopped onion or sliced, hardcooked eggs. Delicious for cocktail canapés and also used in some Smörgåsbord dishes.

Lingonberries are often suggested as a relish for fried meat and fish dishes as well as desserts, puddings, and the like. Lingonberries are the "wild cranberries" of the northern countries, similar in flavor to their first cousin, the cultivated cranberry, but with a different, more subtle taste. Lingonberries, boiled or mixed raw with sugar, are imported to the U.S. and are available on the shelves of an increasing number of food stores. They are mostly packed in 1 pound jars. Lingonberries themselves are an excellent dessert served with cream or milk and hardtack.

9

Swedish Crisp Bread or hardtack, native name *Knäckebröd*, is indispensable with the Smörgåsbord and suggested as an ideal accompaniment to various dishes in this book. In Sweden it is on the table at every meal. It is imported to the U.S. in varieties of light and brown, in 8-oz. packages or other sizes, and sold in many general food stores as well as in Scandinavian specialty shops.

Dill is heavily leaned upon in Swedish cooking where it lends its exquisite, fragrant flavor primarily to fish, but also to some meat dishes, sauces, salads, etc. In the U.S. it is mostly known in connection with dill pickles where only the dill crowns are used. In Sweden dill sprigs are the favored part of this delicate herb, both as garnish and ingredient. New potatoes are enhanced by boiling with dill sprigs. Sources of supply for fresh dill are not too scarce in large cities like New York, but may be difficult to find elsewhere. Dried dill is found in many grocery stores and spice shops.

How to Serve and Enjoy the
Smörgåsbord

Smörgåsbord is the ideal form of entertaining for today's home-maker who wants to fulfill the double task of being the relaxed, charming hostess, and at the same time give her guests a lavish and gustatory treat. This may sound like a paradox to those aquainted with the overrich, sumptuous Smörgåsbord served in some Swedish restaurants and on board Swedish liners. Smörgåsbord is also featured in many restaurants abroad, often in a rather free inter-pretation, except for some genuine Swedish places. But Smörgås-bord is an extremely versatile form of entertaining, highly adaptable to our modern way of life. The "tricks of the trade" will be revealed to you here.

THE CLASSICAL SMÖRGÅSBORD

Smörgåsbord literally means bread-and-butter table. It is said to have originated long ago at rural pot-luck parties to which all the participants brought some dish. Their contributions, together with what the host had to offer, was displayed on a large table from which everybody could help himself to his heart's delight.

To "wet the appetite", the Smörgåsbord invariably starts with herring, both spicy tidbits in cans, of which there is a great assort-ment available in Sweden, and one or more homemade variations. It is served with small, boiled potatoes, chopped chives or onion, and sour cream. Other cold fish and shellfish plates are canned sardines, smoked salmon, smoked eel, cold boiled salmon with mayonnaise, cooked shrimp, lobster salad, fish in aspic, etc. A variety of cold cuts such as ham, salami and other sausages, liver paté or tongue, are also included. In addition there may be cold dishes, such as jellied game bird or stuffed eggs.

11

Hot dishes follow: herring au gratin, small juicy meatballs, sautéed mushrooms and kidneys, one or more fluffy omelets filled with creamed asparagus, sweetbreads, shellfish or other filling.

Cucumber salad, fruit salad, radishes. tomatoes, and other relishes are offered as an accompaniment. The whole meal is topped off with several kinds of cheese.

Bread is as important as other food and present in many varieties, such as *limpa* (Swedish rye bread made with molasses), toast, pumpernickel, two or more types of *knäckebröd* (hardtack/crisp bread) and crackers. The Smörgåsbord can be followed by a main course, dessert and coffee, or merely the latter.

THE ETIQUETTE OF EATING

The art of eating the Smörgåsbord is to pick and choose – but not at random! Just as the correctly composed Smörgåsbord is a well-organized abundance, the Smörgåsbord habitué organizes his eating. Only then is it a true epicurean delight.

The foods should be enjoyed in the proper order as listed above. You may sample as many dishes as you want – in small portions to avoid eating to excess – or stick to a few favorites. Take your time to enjoy everything to the fullest, and make any number of trips to the Smörgåsbord. There is no point in overloading your plate. When it seems appropriate, change your plate for a clean one. The various foods should not mix too much.

With the introductory herring appetizers, *snaps* (aquavite) or fruit juice is generally taken. Beer and slightly carbonated bottled water is served all through the meal, but never wine. The varieties of dishes and flavors are too great to make wine a suitable beverage.

TODAY'S HOME VERSION OF THE SMÖRGÅSBORD

The classical Smörgåsbord as presented above is rarely served in Swedish homes today. It does not go along very well with the current trend to eat less even at festive occasions. Nevertheless, the Smörgåsbord has enjoyed a revival in the last couple of decades. The informal buffet-type of serving is growing in popularity in Sweden as in many other countries where domestic help is rare.

Here the Smörgåsbord comes in very handy. So the Swedish home-maker often resorts to the Smörgåsbord in a more or less trimmed-down version. It can always be assembled in advance, inasmuch as so many of its foods are served cold. Some of them, such as herring tidbits and cold cuts, are purchased at the delicatessen counter. Others such as marinated herring salads, jellies, etc., can be made ahead of time. Even among the hot dishes you can choose those which can be made in advance and just need some last-minute heating, such as meatballs, herring au gratin and fillings for omelets. Listed in the recipe sections of this book are many veterans among Smörgåsbord dishes. You can easily make your own "personalized" Smörgåsbord, and at the same time give it a genuine Swedish touch by choosing from the recipes here. They are carefully selected to represent the highlights of the authentic Swedish Smörgåsbord. Their use is by no means limited to the Smörgåsbord. They can all be served separately at other occasions. The cold plates are excellent appetizers. The hot dishes are delicious luncheon or late supper treats.

GLAMOUR IMPORTANT

Large or small, the Smörgåsbord is always presented in a very attractive way. The homemaker puts to work her artistry in food by making every single plate as enticing as possible in order to give the whole display an impression of limitless culinary delight. A Smörgåsbord party automatically takes on an atmosphere of informality and friendship, with the guests moving around the table and helping themselves to delectable morsels. A genuine Swedish concoction among the dishes you offer will constitute a conversation piece. It will always score the hostess a real success!

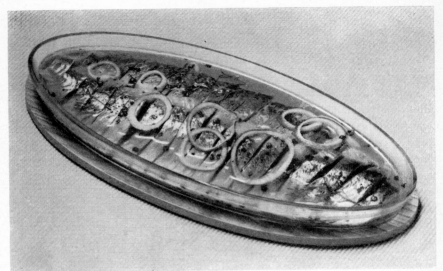

Pickled Salt Herring   *Inlagd sill*

COLD SMÖRGÅSBORD DISHES

Pickled Herring (Marinated Salt Herring)   *Inlagd sill*

1 salt herring (about 1 lb.)
Dressing:
1/2 cup white vinegar
1/4 cup sugar
2 tbsp. chopped onion

6 peppercorns, crushed
6 whole allspice, crushed
Garnish:
onion, chives or dill

Fillet fish and soak overnight in cold water in cool place, preferably refrigerator. Remove small bones and skin. Rinse and drain. Cut crosswise into thin slices. Mix ingredients for dressing. Let stand 10 min. and pour over. Garnish with onion, chives, or dill, see picture. Leave in refrigerator 2–3 hours or overnight.

Chef's Marinated Herring   *Glasmästarsill*

2 salt herring (about 1/2 lb. each)
1 tsp. whole allspice, crushed
2 bay leaves
2 small pieces whole ginger

1/2 tsp. mustard seed
1 small piece horseradish, diced
2 red onions, sliced
1/2 carrot, sliced

14

Dressing:

3/4 cup white vinegar   1/2 cup sugar

Clean fish, but do not fillet, and soak overnight in cold water in cool place, preferably refrigerator. Rinse and drain. Cut crosswise in 1/2″ slices and layer with dry ingredients in glass jar.

Mix vinegar and sugar and bring to the boiling point. Chill. Pour over herring and let stand 3 days in refrigerator.

Serve from jar on Smörgåsbord or as an appetizer with boiled potatoes, if desired.

Bird's Nest   *Fågelbo*

8 Swedish anchovy fillets,   1/3 cup chopped chives and
   chopped (marinated sprats in   parsley, mixed
   can)   1/4 cup diced pickled beets
2 tbsp. chopped onion   2 raw egg yolks
2 tbsp. capers

Place two egg cups upside down in center of serving plate. Arrange anchovy, onion, capers, chives, parsley and beets in circles around cups. Remove egg cups and replace with the two egg yolks, see picture. Serve as an appetizer with toast and butter. The first person to help himself from the dish mixes all ingredients together until well blended.

Bird's Nest   *Fågelbo*

Herring Salad *Sillsallad*

Herring Salad *Sillsallad*

1 salt herring (about 1 lb.)
$1^1/_2$ cups diced boiled potatoes
$1^1/_2$ cups diced pickled beets
$1/_3$ cup diced pickled cucumber
$1/_2$ cup diced apple
$1/_4$ cup chopped onion
$1/_2$ cup heavy cream, optional

Dressing:
$1/_4$ cup vinegar
2 tbsp. sugar
dash of pepper
Garnish:
hard-boiled eggs
parsley

Fillet fish and soak overnight in cold water in cool place, preferably in refrigerator. Remove small bones and skin. Rinse and drain. Dice herring. Mix all ingredients for salad in large bowl thoroughly but carefully. Shake all ingredients for dressing. Let stand a few minutes and pour over. Blend gently. If desired, $1/_2$ cup whipped cream may be added. Pack into glass bowl or mold, rinsed in cold water. Chill in refrigerator.

Serve as Smörgåsbord dish from bowl or unmolded, garnished with hardcooked eggs and parsley or with $1/_2$ cup sour cream beaten stiff and colored with brine from pickled beets.

16

Swedish Caviar Dip

Kaviargrädde

²/₃ cup heavy cream

3 tbsp. Swedish caviar
(Cod roe spread)

2 tbsp. finely chopped onion

Whip cream. Stir in caviar and onion. Chill and serve with potato chips, crackers, or toast.

Stuffed Eggs

Fyllda ägghalvor

4 hard-boiled eggs

1 tbsp. butter

3 tbsp. Swedish caviar
(Cod roe spread)

salt, pepper

Garnish:

parsley, tomatoes

Cut eggs into halves crosswise or lengthwise. Remove yolks carefully and place whites on serving platter lined with lettuce leaves.
Mix egg yolks, butter and caviar and stir until smooth. Season to taste. Force through pastry tube into whites. Decorate each egg with a sprig of dill or parsley. Garnish with sliced tomatoes.

Stuffed Eggs

Fyllda ägghalvor

Jellied Sardines or
Smelts

Inkokt strömming

Marinated Sardines or Smelts   *Marinerad strömming*

2 lb. smelts, sardines (fresh,   dash of pepper
   not canned), or small herring   1 tsp. French mustard
3 tbsp. chopped dill sprigs $1/4$ cup olive oil
Dressing: $1/2$ cup white vinegar
$1^1/2$ tsp. salt   *Garnish:*
1 tbsp. sugar   dill sprigs

Clean fish and remove bones and skin. Rinse and drain.
Sprinkle dill on bottom of a bowl and alternate layers of fish and dill.
Mix all ingredients for dressing and pour over fish. Let stand in
refrigerator 3–4 hours.
Garnish with dill sprigs and serve with boiled potatoes on Smörgåsbord or as appetizer.
6 servings.

Jellied Sardines or Smelts   *Inkokt strömming i gelé*

2 lb. smelts, sardines (fresh,   5 whole allspice
   not canned) or small herring   1 bay leaf
dill sprigs $1^1/2$ tsp. salt
Aspic: dill sprigs
$3/4$ cup white vinegar   1 envelope unflavored gelatin
$3/4$ cup water $1/4$ cup cold water
5 peppercorns

Clean fish, remove backbone. Rinse and drain. Place one dill sprig on each fish and roll up tight. Place rolls close together in low saucepan. Bring aspic ingredients to boil, pour over fish and simmer 6–8 min., gently, to avoid fish falling into pieces.

Remove fish carefully to mold. Strain stock. Soften gelatin in cold water. Add to 2 cups of hot stock and stir until dissolved. Pour over fish. Chill until set. Unmold on platter. (If difficult, dip mold an instant in hot water.) Serve as Smörgåsbord or luncheon dish.
6 servings.

Lobster Salad   *Hummersallad*

about 1 cup (6½-oz. can)   1–1½ cups small peas
    lobster meat   ½ cup mayonnaise
about 1 cup (5-oz. can)   ½ cup heavy cream
    asparagus tips   lettuce leaves
1 cup thinly sliced celery

Drain lobster meat and slice. Drain asparagus and peas. Blend mayonnaise and whipped cream.

Layer all ingredients in deep serving bowl. Garnish with nice pieces of lobster meat, asparagus, and lettuce. Chill. 4–6 servings.

Variation: One boiled lobster may be substituted for canned lobster.

Lobster Salad   *Hummersallad*

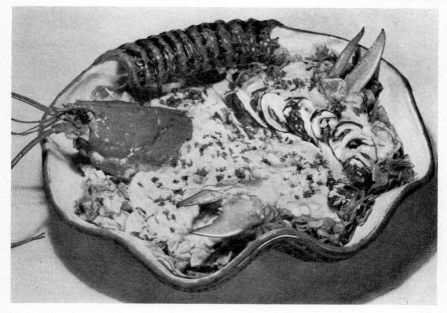

Eggs with Mayonnaise and Shrimp   *Ägg i majonnäs med räkor*

4 hard-boiled eggs
1¹/₂ cups peeled shrimp
¹/₂ cup mayonnaise
¹/₂ cup heavy cream
salt, pepper

Garnish:
2 tbsp. chopped chives or dill
sprigs

Cut eggs into halves and place in center of serving dish. Arrange shrimp around eggs. Whip cream and stir into mayonnaise. Season. Pour over eggs. Garnish with chives or dill.
Serve as Smörgåsbord or luncheon dish.
4 servings.

HOT SMÖRGÅSBORD DISHES

Jansson's Temptation
(Swedish Anchovies au Gratin)

Janssons Frestelse

2 onions, sliced
3 tbsp. butter
4 medium raw potatoes, peeled
    and cut into small strips

about 20 Swedish anchovy fillets
    (Marinated sprats in can)
1¹/₄ cups cream

Sauté onion in 1 tbsp. of butter. Butter baking dish. Layer potatoes, onion, and anchovy fillets, finishing with layer of potatoes. Pour over 1 tbsp. of brine from anchovy can and dot with remaining butter. Add half of cream. Bake in hot oven (400°F.) 50–60 min. Add remaining cream after 10 min. baking time. Serve hot from baking dish.
4–6 servings.

Herring au Gratin

Sillgratäng

1 or 2 salt herring
6 medium raw potatoes, peeled
    and thinly sliced
2 onions, sliced

dash of white pepper
2 tbsp. bread crumbs
4 tbsp. butter

Fillet fish and soak overnight in cold water, preferably in refrigerator. Drain. Remove skin and small bones. Cut fillets in halves lengthwise.

Continued on p. 22.

Preparing Jansson's Temptation

Janssons Frestelse

Preparing Herring au Gratin

Sillgratäng

Arrange herring, potatoes, and onion in buttered baking dish in alternate rows, see picture. Sprinkle with pepper and bread crumbs and dot with butter. Bake in very hot oven (450°F.) 50–60 min. or until potatoes are soft. Serve hot from baking dish.
4–6 servings.

Swedish Caviar Custard *Kaviarlåda*

1 cup cream
3 tbsp. bread crumbs
3 tbsp. (3¹/₂-oz. can) Swedish caviar (Cod roe spread)
3 eggs

3 tbsp. chopped chives or dill sprigs
1 tbsp. butter

Heat cream to the boiling point and pour over bread crumbs. Stir in caviar, eggs, and chives. Pour mixture into buttered baking dish and dot with butter. Bake in hot oven (400°F.) 25 min. Serve hot from baking dish.
4 servings.

Baked Fresh Sardines or Smelts *Strömmingslåda*

2 lb. sardines (fresh, not canned) or small herring, or smelts
1¹/₂ tsp. salt, optional

12 Swedish anchovy fillets (Marinated sprats in can)
2 tbsp. butter
2 tbsp. bread crumbs

Clean fish. Remove heads tails, entrails, and bones. Rinse. Drain on absorbent paper. Sprinkle with salt.
Cut each anchovy fillet in 2 pieces. Place one piece on each fish and roll tight.
Place rolls in well buttered baking dish. Pour 1 tbsp. brine from anchovy can over fish, dot with remaining butter and sprinkle with bread crumbs. Bake in hot oven (425°F.) 20–25 min., or until golden brown. Serve from baking dish as Smörgåsbord dish or as main course with boiled or fried potatoes and lettuce salad.

Swedish caviar (Cod roe spread) may be substituted for anchovies. Mix about 3 tbsp. (half of contents of 3¹/₂-oz. can) caviar with 2 tbsp. butter until creamy and spread on fish before rolling it up. Bake as above.
6 servings.

22

Preparing Baked Fresh Sardines   *Strömmingslåda*

Cheese Soufflé   *Ostsufflé*

2 tbsp. butter
3 tbsp. flour
1 cup milk
1 cup grated cheese
3 egg yolks
5 egg whites
salt, pepper

Melt butter. Stir in flour and, gradually, milk. Simmer until thick,
stirring occasionally. Remove from heat and let cool for a few minutes.
Beat egg yolks and stir into sauce. Blend in cheese. Season to taste.
Beat egg whites until stiff and fold into batter.
Pour batter into buttered baking dish. Sprinkle with cheese. Bake in
slow oven (325°F.) until set, about 50 min. Serve immediately from
baking dish.
4 servings.

23

24

TYPICAL SMÖRGÅSBORD FOR CHRISTMAS EVE SUPPER
is pictured on the colorspread found between pages 24 and 25.

Top row: Various Types of Bread; Chef's Marinated Herring; Herring Salad; Cheeses; Pork Sausage; "Dip in the Kettle"; Smörgåsbord Meatballs; Roast Spareribs; Jellied Veal; Head Cheese.

Bottom row: Pickled Beets and Pickled Cucumbers; Liver Paté Loaf; Christmas Ham; Browned Red Cabbage; Creamed Kale; Cold Cuts.

Background: Coffee Table.

CANAPÉS

1st row: Swedish Anchovy with Sour Cream; Caviar; Swedish Anchovy and Hard-Boiled Egg; Smoked Eel with Scrambled Egg; Salmon Caviar.

2nd row: Salmon Caviar and Egg on Lettuce; Smoked Salmon and Asparagus; Smoked Salmon and Dill; Layer Sandwich; Smoked Eel and Cucumber.

3rd row: Shrimp with Mayonnaise; Sliced Tongue with Vegetable Salad; Smoked Reindeer Meat and Egg Pudding; Fruit Salad Sandwiches; Shrimp and Dill Sprig.

4th row: Beef Roast with Pickled Onions; Boiled Ham with Pineapple; Liver Paté Spread with Olives; Sliced Tongue with Whipped Cream mixed with Grated Horseradish; Sliced Ham with Apple and Beet Salad.

5th row: Fruit Salad Sandwich; Blue Cheese on Chopped Radishes; Cheese Spread with Grapes; Camembert Cheese with Radishes; Fruit Sandwich.

Meatballs before and after Frying

Köttbullar

Smörgåsbord Meatballs   *Små köttbullar*

There are two types of Swedish meatballs. The regular ones, served as main course, see recipe p. 52, and the tiny ones, never missing on the Smörgåsbord, and also appreciated as a cocktail tidbit.

1/3 cup bread crumbs	1/4 lb. ground pork
1 cup water and cream, mixed	1 1/2 tsp. salt
1 tbsp. butter	1/4 tsp. pepper
1 tbsp. finely chopped onion	*To fry:*
3/4 lb. ground beef	2 tbsp. butter

Preparation as for Swedish Meatballs, see recipe p. 52, but the Smörgåsbord meatballs should be of only half the size. Shape them with one hand and a teaspoon, dipped in cold water.
Brown butter in skillet and fry meatballs in batches of 15 to 20 until evenly brown, shaking pan continuously to make balls round.
Serve hot or cold as Smörgåsbord dish or on toothpicks with cocktail.
Makes about 100 meatballs.

Oven Omelet with Filling   *Ugnsomelett med fyllning*

4 eggs	1 1/3 cups cream or milk
1/2 tsp. salt	1 tbsp. butter
dash of pepper	

Beat eggs slightly with seasonings and add cream. Pour into buttered baking dish. Bake in moderate oven (350°F.) 25–30 min. or until set. Pour over omelet: Creamed Mushrooms (recipe p. 27), Creamed Lobster (recipe p. 27), Creamed Sweetbread (recipe p. 43), or creamed asparagus. Garnish with chopped parsley. Serve hot from baking dish.

Variations: Add 1 cup cubed smoked ham or 2 tbsp. chopped chives or parsley to omelet batter. Omit other filling. 4 servings.

Fluffy Omelet with Filling   *Fylld Musslinomelett*

5 eggs

1 tsp. salt

2 tbsp. cream

To fry:

1 tbsp. butter

Beat egg yolks and salt. Add cream. Carefully fold in stiffly beaten egg whites.
Melt butter in omelet pan over slow heat. Pour batter into pan. Shake pan lightly over low heat to keep omelet from sticking. When set, remove to serving dish. Pour over omelet: Creamed Mushrooms (recipe below), Creamed Lobster (recipe below), or creamed asparagus. Garnish with chopped parsley. Serve immediately.
6 servings.

Creamed Mushrooms   *Svampstuvning*

1/2 lb. fresh mushrooms, sliced, or 5-oz. can mushrooms, drained

2 tbsp. butter

1/2 tsp. salt

dash of pepper

2 tbsp. flour

1³/4 cups cream and stock if canned mushrooms are used

1 tbsp. dry sherry, optional

Melt butter and sauté mushrooms over low heat 5 min. Season. Stir in flour and add stock and cream gradually. Simmer 5 min., stirring occasionally. Season and add wine. Serve as filling in omelet or in pastry shells.
4 servings.

Creamed Lobster   *Hummerstuvning*

1 cup (5¹/2-oz. can) lobster meat

2 tbsp. butter

2 tbsp. flour

1¹/4 cups lobster stock and cream

2 tbsp. dry sherry, optional

salt, cayenne pepper

Drain lobster meat and cut into chunks. Melt butter, add flour and stir until well blended. Gradually stir in stock and cream. Simmer 5 min., stirring occasionally. Remove from heat, add lobster meat and wine. Season. Heat quickly, but do not boil.
Serve in omelet or pastry shells.

Shrimp, crayfish, or crabmeat may be substituted for lobster.
4 servings.

27

Thursday dinner: Yellow Pea Soup with Pork
followed by Pancakes with Jam

Ärter med fläsk,
Pannkakor med sylt

Five Hearty Soups

In old time Sweden, substantial soups of the type that constitutes a meal in itself were a cornerstone in the farmer's diet especially. To satisfy the sturdy appetite of hard-working people, some starch-rich dessert like porridge, pancakes, or the like was often added. Along the coasts rich fish chowders were a regular standby.

In Sweden today all kinds of soups known from the international kitchen are eaten. A delectable consommé, cream, or bisque is a common overture to the festive dinner or banquet. Canned soups of all kinds have renewed the position of soup in the daily eating.

For a few oldtimers which are still great favorites with practically everybody, recipes are given here in their seasonal sequence:

Nettle Soup, the pleasant spring soup, based upon the first tender shoots of the nettle. In preparation and looks, it comes close to spinach soup but has a unique flavor;

Summer Vegetable Soup, based upon the fresh summer vegetables when they are at their peak in fragrance and tenderness;

Browned Cabbage Soup with Veal Dumplings, is all-winter fare but at its best in the early fall when the cabbage is fresh and yong;

Yellow Pea Soup with Pork, still on the menu in many homes and restaurants every Thursday during wintertime, and traditionally followed by the small thin Swedish pancakes with jam, see picture, p. 28. It is nowadays often bought readymade, since it gains in fulness and flavor by being prepared in large batches;

Clear Beef Soup with Almond Dumplings, which also retains its status as a rich and wholesome food.

Nettle Soup *Nässelkål*

2 qt. very young nettles
2 cups water
1 tsp. salt
1/4 cup chopped chives
1 tbsp. butter

1¹/₂ tbsp. flour
2 cups beef stock and cooking
   liquid from nettles
salt, pepper

Wash nettles well and drain. Cook in water with salt 10 min. or until soft. Strain, reserving liquid. Chop nettles and chives finely or pass through sieve. Melt butter, add flour and stir until well blended. Add stock, still stirring, and simmer 5 min. Add nettles and reheat. Season. Serve with poached eggs or hard-boiled eggs cut in halves or sections. 4 servings.

Summer Soup *Ängamat*

1/2 head cauliflower, cut in
   sections
1/2 lb. green peas in shells
4 small carrots, sliced
6 cups water
1 tsp. salt

1/4 tsp. pepper
1 tbsp. butter
2 tbsp. flour
1 egg yolk
1/3 cup light cream

Cook vegetables until tender in salted water. Mix butter and flour carefully and add to soup. Simmer 5 min., stirring. Beat egg yolk and cream together in soup tureen. Pour hot soup over, stirring gently. Season.
Sprinkle with chopped parsley and serve with cheese and Swedish crisp bread or crackers.
4 servings.

Browned Cabbage Soup *Vitkålssoppa*

1¹/₂ lb. white cabbage
1/4 cup fat or butter
3/4 tbsp. dark corn syrup
6 cups beef and vegetable stock

6 whole allspice
6 white peppercorns
salt

Trim cabbage and cube, discarding core and tough portions. Brown in fat. Add syrup when cabbage is lightly brown and continue to cook for a few minutes, stirring constantly.

Heat stock in saucepan. Add cabbage. Season. Simmer, covered, until cabbage is soft, for new cabbage about 30 min. Serve with Veal Dumplings, see recipe below, or with boiled sausages.
4 servings.

Veal Dumplings for Cabbage Soup   *Frikadeller*

1/2 cup milk	*To cook:*
1 tbsp. bread crumbs	1 qt. water
1/4 lb. ground veal	11/2 tsp. salt
1/4 lb. ground pork	
1 tbsp. grated onion	
1 tsp. cornstarch	
1 tsp. salt	
dash of white pepper	

Soak bread crumbs in half of milk. Mix remaining ingredients. Blend in bread crumbs and milk gradually. Shape batter into balls, 1/2 walnut size, and boil 5 min. in salted water or in cabbage soup.
4 servings.

Yellow Pea Soup with Pork   *Ärter med fläsk*

11/2 cups dried yellow Swedish	*To cook:*
peas	2 qts. water
To soak:	(2 tsp. salt)
2 qts. water	1 lb. lightly salted side pork
2 tbsp. salt	1 onion
	1 tsp. marjoram or 1/2 tsp.
	ginger

Rinse peas. Soak them overnight in salted water. Rinse again. Turn peas into saucepan. Add water. Cover and bring quickly to the boiling point. Remove shells floating on top of water. Add pork and onion and seasonings. Cover and simmer until pork and peas are tender (1–11/2 hours). Add salt if necessary. Remove pork. Cut in slices and serve separately with mustard. See picture, p. 28.
4 servings.

Clear Beef Soup with Dumplings   *Köttsoppa med klimp*

2 lb. chuck, shanks, or   1 piece celery root (2 ounces)
    shoulder of beef   1 onion
2 qts. water   5 parsley sprigs
1 tsp. salt   1 bay leaf
2 carrots   6 whole allspice
1 parsnip   *To clear:*
1 leek   2 egg whites to every qt. stock

Rinse meat in cold running water and cut in large cubes. Crack bones, place in large kettle, add meat and cold water. Cover and heat slowly to the boiling point. Skim. Add vegetables and spices and again bring to boil. Remove scum carefully, cover and let simmer 3 hours. Strain through double cheesecloth. Chill stock and store stock in refrigerator. To clear, remove fat from stock, place slightly beaten egg whites in kettle and add cold stock. Bring slowly to the boiling point, stirring constantly and boil 2 min. Let stand covered 20 min. Strain through several layers of cheesecloth. Heat and serve with Almond Dumplings, see recipe below. Meat can be used for Swedish Hash, see recipe p. 56. 4 servings.

Almond Dumplings   *Klimp*

1¹/₂ tbsp. butter   1 tsp. sugar
¹/₄ cup flour   1 tbsp. ground almond and
1¹/₂–2 cups milk   1 tsp. almond extract
2 egg yolks   or 5 cardamon seeds, pounded

Melt butter, add flour and stir until well blended. Gradually stir in milk. Simmer 5 min., stirring occasionally. Remove from heat, add slightly beaten egg yolks and reheat but do not boil, stirring constantly. Add sugar, almonds, almond extract or cardamon. Pour into bowl rinsed in cold water. Refrigerate 1–2 hours. Garnish with shredded almonds or chopped parsley. Serve with Clear Beef Soup, see above.

Meat Dishes

Both pork, beef, veal and lamb are used in the Swedish kitchen, possibly with some preference for pork. As the recipes that follow here show, they are all prepared in ingenious ways. The most prevalent meat product of the country are various types of sausages which have an old tradition behind them. The most popular type is the so-called *falukorv*, named after an old mining city, Falun, and almost a weekly dish in most homes, as common as hamburgers in the United States. Chicken is party food and increasingly so in recent years, thanks to greater availability. Goose is honored as a special treat at a particular Fall celebration.

Reindeer meat is the staple diet of the Laplanders in the Far North, but cherished all over the country, particularly as smoked cold cuts – a superb delicacy which no visitor to Sweden could afford to miss. The Lapps have many reindeer specialties, among others a sturdy wholesome marrow-bone soup.

With half of its surface covered by forests, it is only natural that Sweden should have a good supply of game and fowl. The elk, "King of the Forest", is the best meat provider, and various cuts are prepared much the same way as with beef. Deer, venison and hare are common. Fowl is richly represented by pheasants, partridges, white grouses, capercailzies, woodcocks, and snipes. They are first epicurean choice for festive occasions. Their individual aromas are brought out through a skillfull preparation.

Veal Pot Roast used to be the regular Sunday family dinner and is still highly popular. Beef roast was earlier often marinated in milk or wine and this is still being done to some extent. Pork is preferably stuffed with prunes and apples. To get the most and the best out of less expensive cuts, casserole cooking and boiling is practiced.

Opulent sauces go with many dishes, in some cases with dill or horseradish as aroma-giving agents. The Swedes make judicious use of spices and herbs in their meat cookery – an art in which they owe a great deal to the French and other European cuisines. Tournedo, Chateaubriand, Filet Mignon, Wienerschnitzel, and many other foreign specialities are incorporated into the common recipe treasure. Minced meat dishes are plentiful, with the internationally famous Swedish meatballs as stars.

SWEDISH WAYS WITH BEEF

Royal Pot Roast of Beef   *Slottsstek*

4 lb. round or rump of beef
$1^1/_2$ tsp. salt
$^1/_2$ tsp. pepper
2 tbsp. butter
2 cups stock or water
2 onions
4 Swedish anchovy fillets
    (marinated sprats in can)
2 bay leaves
$^1/_2$ tsp. whole allspice
$^1/_2$ tsp. white peppercorns

2 tbsp. vinegar
2 tbsp. brandy, optional
1 tbsp. dark corn syrup,
    optional
Gravy:
2 cups pan drippings and stock
3 tbsp. flour
$^1/_4$ cup water or stock
1 cup light cream
salt, pepper
1 tbsp. anchovy brine from can

Rub meat with salt and pepper. Brown butter in Dutch oven or heavy kettle. Add meat and brown on all sides. Add water or stock and all remaining ingredients. Cover and cook slowly on top of stove for about 3 hours or until tender. When done, place on hot platter and keep warm.
Strain pan drippings. Measure and add enough stock to make 2 cups. Heat. Blend flour with small amount of water. Stir into drippings. Add cream gradually and simmer 5 min. Season with salt, pepper, and anchovy brine.
Slice roast and serve with gravy and vegetables and Browned Potatoes, see picture, p. 35.
8 servings.

Royal Pot Roast

Slottsstek

Browned Beef Stew

Kalops

2 lb. beef chuck
2 tsp. salt
$1/4$ tsp. pepper
3 tbsp. flour
2 tbsp. butter
3 onions, cut in sections
10–15 whole allspice
2 bay leaves
2 cups hot water

Cut meat into large cubes and remove sinews.
Combine in paper bag, flour, salt and pepper. Add meat and shake well.
Heat butter in heavy skillet and brown onion and meat on all sides.
Add seasonings and boiling water. Cover and simmer $1–1^1/_2$ hours, or until meat is done. Stir occasionally. Add more water if needed.
Serve with boiled potatoes and pickled beets or lingonberries.
6 servings.

35

Sailor's Beef Casserole   *Sjömansbiff*

1¹/₂ lb. chuck or round of beef
6 medium raw potatoes
3 tbsp. butter
2 large onions, sliced
1¹/₂ tsp. salt
dash of pepper

1¹/₂ cups hot water
¹/₂ cup beer
¹/₄ cup chopped parsley

Cut meat into ¹/₄ inch thick slices and pound. Peel potatoes and cut in thick slices. Heat butter; sauté onion and brown meat. Layer potatoes, meat, and onion in casserole and sprinkle between layers with salt and pepper. The top layer should be potatoes. Pour water into frying pan, stir and add liquid to casserole. Add beer. Cover and cook in moderate oven (375°F.) 1–1¹/₂ hours or until meat is tender. Sprinkle with chopped parsley and serve from casserole with pickled beets. 4 servings.

Boiled Beef with Horseradish Sauce   *Pepparrotskött med sås*

2 to 2¹/₂ lb. chuck or brisket
of beef
To every qt. water:
1 carrot
1 small parsnip

1 small piece celery root
1 onion, chopped
1 tbsp. salt
5 whole allspice
1 bay leaf

Place meat in kettle and barely cover with water. Bring to the boiling point and skim.
Add vegetables; bring to the boiling point. Skim. Add salt and allspice and simmer about 2 hours or until meat is tender.
Slice meat and place on hot platter. Garnish with vegetables and shredded horseradish. Serve with boiled potatoes and Horseradish Sauce, see below. 4 servings.

Horseradish Sauce for Boiled Beef   *Pepparrotssås*

1¹/₂ tbsp. butter
2 tbsp. flour
1 cup beef stock

1 cup milk
2–3 tbsp. grated horseradish
salt, pepper

Melt butter and blend in flour. Gradually stir in milk and stock. Simmer 5 min., stirring occasionally. Season. Add grated horseradish. Do not boil sauce after adding horseradish or flavor will be bitter.

Preparing Beef Rolls

Oxrulader

Braised Beef Rolls

Oxrulader

2 lb. round beef, in $1/4$ inch
thick slices
$1/4$ lb. fat pork or bacon,
cut in strips
1 tsp. salt
$1/4$ tsp. pepper

2 tbsp. flour
2 tbsp. butter
1 bouillon cube dissolved in
$1/2$ cup boiling water
$1/4$ cup cream

Pound meat lightly. Sprinkle with salt and pepper. Place one strip fat
on each slice of beef and roll up, securing with string or toothpick.
Coat rolls with flour. Heat butter in heavy skillet and brown rolls on
all sides. Add bouillon and season. Simmer covered 1 hour or until
meat is tender, turning rolls occasionally. Remove strings or toothpicks
and place rolls in hot, deep serving dish. Add cream to gravy, bring
to the boiling point, stirring, and pour over rolls. Serve with boiled
or fried potatoes, cucumber and pickled beets.
4 servings.

Swedish Steak with Onions   *Biff med lök*

Swedish Steak with Onions   *Biffstek med lök*

 2 lb. (4 slices) rump or top 4 onions, sliced
  round of beef or sirloin steak salt, pepper
 3 tbsp. butter $^{1}/_{2}$ cup boiling water

Pound meat lightly. Melt part of butter in frying pan and sauté onion
until tender and nicely brown. Remove and keep warm. Add remaining
butter to pan and brown. Season meat and fry 2 to 3 min. on each
side or longer if desired.
Remove meat to hot platter. Place onions on top. Pour boiling water
into frying pan. Heat and stir. Pour over steaks. Serve hot with fried
potatoes.
4 servings.

Beef Tongue with Mushroom Sauce   *Oxtunga med svampsås*

 1 fresh beef tongue ($2^{1}/_{2}$ lb.) $^{1}/_{2}$ tsp. white peppercorns
 water 1 bay leaf
 2 tbsp. salt 1 carrot
 $^{1}/_{2}$ tsp. whole allspice 1 small onion

38

Rinse tongue in cold water.

Place in water, add salt and bring to the boiling point. Skim. Add remaining ingredients and simmer 2–2½ hours or until done.

Remove skin while tongue is still warm. Cut in thin slices and arrange on hot platter. Garnish with tomatoes and parsley and serve with boiled or mashed potatoes, peas, and Mushroom Sauce, see below.

Tongue is delicious served cold. After removal of skin, let tongue cool in stock. It should always be stored in its stock.

6 servings.

Mushroom Sauce for Ox Tongue   *Svampsås*

½ lb. fresh mushrooms or one
    5-oz. can mushrooms, drained
½ tsp. salt
dash of pepper
2 tbsp. butter

2 tbsp. flour
2 cups cream and stock, if
    canned mushrooms are used
salt, pepper
1 tbsp. sherry, optional

Melt butter, add mushrooms and seasonings and cook over low heat 5–10 min. Gradually add flour, stock and cream stirring constantly. Simmer 5 min., stirring occasionally. Season. Add sherry.

4 servings.

SWEDISH WAYS WITH VEAL
LAMB, POULTRY

Veal Pot Roast   *Kalvstek*

5 lb. leg or round or rump
    of veal
2 tbsp. butter
1 tbsp. salt
½ tsp. pepper
1½ cups bouillon
    or hot water

Gravy:
3 tbsp. flour
2 cups pan drippings and stock
½ cup light cream
salt, pepper

Heat butter in Dutch oven or heavy kettle and brown meat on all sides. Sprinkle with salt and pepper. Add liquid and cook slowly, covered, 1½–2 hours or until meat is done. Remove roast to hot serving platter and keep warm.

Continued next page.

Veal Pot Roast   *Kalvstek*

Strain pan drippings. Measure and add stock to make 2 cups liquid.
Heat. Blend flour with small amount of water. Stir into liquid. Add
cream gradually and simmer 5 min., stirring occasionally. Season and
serve separately.

Slice roast and garnish with vegetables and serve with Browned
Potatoes, see recipe p. 76, Cucumber Salad, see recipe p. 75, and
lingonberries or jelly.

6–8 servings.

Braised Whole Calf's Liver   *Helstekt kalvlever*

2 lb. calf's liver	*Gravy:*
$1^1/_2$ tsp. salt	2 tbsp. flour
$1/_4$ tsp. pepper	$1/_4$ cup water
2 tbsp. butter	$1^1/_2$ cups pan drippings and
$1^1/_2$ cups water or water	bouillon
and milk	$1/_2$ cup cream
	salt and pepper

Place liver in cold water for 15 min. Trim and drain liver. Rub with salt and pepper. Brown evenly in butter in heavy skillet turning liver with two wooden spoons. Add water, cover, and simmer about 1 hour or until done, basting occasionally. Remove liver, place on hot platter and keep warm.

Measure pan drippings. Mix flour and water and stir into drippings. Add cream. Simmer 5 min., stirring occasionally. Season to taste.

Cut liver in thin slices and pour gravy over. Serve with boiled potatoes, vegetables, lingonberries and Cucumber Salad, recipe p. 75.
6 servings.

Braised Veal Birds   *Kalvkycklingar*

2 lb. veal cutlets cut in 1/4 inch
   slices, pounded
1 tsp. salt
1/4 tsp. pepper
Stuffing:
2 tbsp. butter
3 tbsp. chopped parsley

To fry:
2 tbsp. butter
1 cup water
Gravy:
pan drippings
1 tbsp. flour
2 tbsp. water
1/2 cup cream
salt, pepper

Mix butter and parsley for stuffing. Sprinkle meat on both sides with salt and pepper and spread one side of each slice with stuffing. Roll up and secure with toothpicks or string.

Heat butter in heavy skillet and brown "birds" on all sides. Add part of hot water. Simmer covered 3/4–1 hour or until meat is tender. Baste occasionally, adding more hot water if needed. Remove toothpicks or string, place rolls in hot deep serving dish and keep warm.

Strain pan drippings. Blend flour and water and stir into drippings. Add cream. Simmer 5 min., stirring occasionally. Season and pour gravy over rolls. Serve with boiled potatoes, vegetables, Cucumber Salad, recipe p. 75, and lingonberries.
4 servings.

Kidney Sauté   *Njursauté*

Veal Kidney Sauté   *Njursauté*

1 lb. veal kidney

$^1/_2$ lb. fresh mushrooms or
4-oz. can, optional

1 tbsp. butter

salt, pepper

1 tbsp. flour

$^1/_2$–$^3/_4$ cup beef and mushroom
stock

$^1/_2$ cup cream

2 tbsp. dry sherry

Clean mushrooms and cut into thin slices lengthwise. (Drain canned mushrooms.)

Place kidneys in saucepan and cover with cold water. Heat slowly to the boiling point. Rinse in cold water. Drain well.

Remove most fat and heavy veins from kidney and cut into slices or cubes.

Heat half of butter in skillet, add kidney and brown evenly. Remove to platter. Heat remaining butter and brown mushrooms. Return kidney. Season. Sprinkle flour over mixture and stir until well blended. Gradually add stock and cream, stirring. Simmer 10–15 min., add wine, and season to taste. Serve hot.

4 servings.

42

Fried Sweetbreads   *Stekt kalvbräss*

Creamed Sweetbreads   *Stuvad kalvbräss*

1 lb. sweetbreads	1^1/$_2$ cups sweetbread stock
^{1}/$_2$ tbsp. salt	and cream
2 tbsp. butter	salt, pepper
2 tbsp. flour	a few drops of lemon juice,
	sherry or onion juice

Soak sweetbreads in cold water for 1 hour. Place in fresh, cold, salted water and bring to the boiling point. Rinse in cold water.
Bring 1 quart water to boil, add salt and sweetbreads. Skim. Simmer 15 min.
Remove membranes and tubes and cube sweetbreads.
Melt butter in saucepan, add flour and stir until well blended. Add stock and cream gradually while stirring. Simmer 5 min., stirring occasionally. Season. Add sweetbreads and heat thoroughly. Serve in pastry shells, on toast or as omelet filling. 4 servings.

Fried Sweetbreads   *Stekt kalvbräss*

Prepare sweetbreads as in recipe above. When cold, slice and dip in beaten egg and then in seasoned breadcrumbs. Fry in butter until golden brown on both sides. Serve with green peas.

43

Boiled Lamb or Veal
with Dill Sauce
Lamm- eller Kalvfrikassé

2 to 2¹/₂ lb. breast, leg or
shoulder of lamb or veal

1–1¹/₂ qt. water

2 tsp. salt

5 whole allspice

7 white peppercorns

1 bay leaf

bunch of dill sprigs

Place meat in kettle and cover with boiling water. Bring to boil and skim. Add seasonings. Cover and simmer 1–1¹/₂ hours or until meat is done. Cut meat into pieces, place on hot platter and garnish with dill. Serve with Dill Sauce, see below, and boiled potatoes.
4 servings.

Dill Sauce for Boiled Lamb or Veal
Dillsås

2 tbsp. butter

2 tbsp. flour

1¹/₂ cups stock

2 tbsp. chopped dill sprigs

1 tbsp. vinegar

¹/₂ tbsp. sugar

¹/₄ tsp. salt

1 egg yolk

Melt butter, add flour and stir until well blended. Gradually stir in stock. Simmer 5 min., stirring occasionally. Add dill, vinegar, and sugar. Season to taste. Remove from heat and add beaten egg yolk. Serve immediately.
4 servings.

Lamb in Cabbage
Får i kål

2 lb. shoulder or breast of
lamb cut into large cubes

1 cabbage head (2 lb.)

1 tbsp. salt

10 white peppercorns

2 bay leaves

2 cups water

chopped parsley

Trim cabbage and cut in large pieces. Place layers of meat and cabbage in large heavy saucepan. Sprinkle layers with salt and pepper. Add bay leaves and water, cover and bring to the boiling point. Skim. Simmer 1¹/₂ hour or until meat is tender. Serve sprinkled with parsley and with boiled potatoes.

Variation: If preferred, brown meat in butter and boil in water with seasonings for about 15 min. before adding cabbage. Boil another 30 min. or until meat is done.
4 servings.

44

Fried Chicken Swedish Style   *Stekt kyckling*

Fried Chicken Swedish Style   *Stekt kyckling*

1 broiler-fryer (about 2½ lb.)   *To fry:*
½ lemon   2 tbsp. butter
2–3 tsp. salt   ¼ cup water
¼ tsp. pepper   *Gravy:*
Stuffing: pan drippings
4 tbsp. chopped parsley sprigs   1 cup cream
2 tbsp. butter   chicken livers
                                   salt, pepper

Rub inside of chicken with lemon. Rub inside and out with salt and
pepper. Stuff with parsley and butter. Truss.
Heat butter in heavy kettle and brown chicken on all sides. Add hot
water and cook slowly, covered 30–40 min. or until tender, basting
occasionally.
Strain pan drippings. Gradually add cream and simmer 2 min.,
stirring occasionally. Grate livers and add. Season.
Cut up chicken and place on hot platter. Garnish with tomatoes and
parsley. Serve with Browned Potatoes, recipe p. 76, and lettuce salad.
4 servings.

45

SWEDISH WAYS WITH PORK

Loin of Pork with Prunes

Plommonspäckad fläskkarré

4–5 lb. loin of pork
15 prunes, halved and pitted
2 tsp. salt
$1/2$ tsp. pepper

$1/4$ tsp. ginger, optional
$1/4$ cup prune juice
$2^1/2$ cups water and bouillon
2–3 tbsp. flour

Insert prunes deep into meat, see picture. Rub meat with seasonings and tie into shape with string. Place a meat thermometer in thickest part of meat. Thermometer should not touch bone. Roast uncovered in roasting pan in slow oven (325°F.) about $1^1/2$–2 hours. When thermometer shows 185°F., roast is done.
Place meat on hot platter, remove string, cut away back bone, slice and serve, see picture. Mix together pan drippings, prune juice, and liquid (to make $2^2/3$ cups). Heat. Mix flour with small amount water and stir into mixture. Simmer 5 min., stirring occasionally. Season and add 1 tsp. red currant jelly.
Serve separately.
Serve with Browned Potatoes, recipe p. 76, cooked prunes, apple sauce, and any desired vegetables. 8 servings.

Roasted Spareribs

Ugnstekt revbensspjäll

5 lb. spareribs, meaty and with
   bones cracked about 1" long
$1^1/2$ tbsp. salt
$1/2$ tsp. pepper

$1/4$ tsp. ginger or powdered
   mustard, optional
$1/4$ cup prune juice
$1^3/4$ cups water and bouillon

Trim meat. Mix seasonings and rub meat. Place in roasting pan with meaty side up. Roast in moderate oven (350°F.) for $1^1/2$ hours or until the bones can be loosened from meat. Cover meat with foil if meat gets too brown.
Cut spareribs in pieces and place on hot platter and keep warm.
Mix pan drippings with prune juice, water and bouillon. Season, heat and serve separately along with apple sauce, cooked prunes, Browned Potatoes, p. 76, and vegetables, or serve meat hot or cold as Smörgåsbord dish.

Variation: Roast Spareribs with Prunes and Apples
Halve and pit 20 prunes. Peel, core and slice 3 apples. Rub meat with mixed seasonings. Spread fruit over inside of ribs, roll and tie securely.

Loin of Pork with Prunes   *Plommonspäckad fläskkarré*

Roast as above for 1^1/$_2$ to 2 hours. Carve and place on hot platter garnished with cooked prunes and apples. Mix pan drippings, prune juice, water and bouillon. Season, and serve separately. 6–8 servings.

Oven Pancake with Pork or Bacon   *Fläskpannkaka*

^{3}/$_4$ cup flour   2 eggs
salt, optional   2 cups milk
1 tsp. sugar, optional ^{1}/$_2$ lb. bacon or salt side pork

Sift flour into bowl. Add sugar and salt. Mix eggs and milk and add gradually, stirring until well blended.
Cube bacon or pork and fry in skillet or omelet pan. Beat up batter, pour over pork and bake in hot oven (425°F.) 30 min. or until set and nicely brown. Cut in sections and serve with lingonberries. May also be fried in thin pancakes on top of stove. 4 servings.

Oven Pancake   *Ugnspannkaka*

Prepare as in recipe above omitting pork or bacon. Serve with jam.

47

DESSERTS

From top to bottom: Frying of Thin Swedish Pancakes in Orange-flavored Butter; Apple Dumplings, Rennet Pudding; Cherry Pie; Stuffed Baked Apples.

From top to bottom: Sunday Cake with Vanilla Cream
Filling; Polynées; Checkerboard Cookies; Vanilla Rocks;
Uppåkra Cookies; Almond Wafers.

4

Fried Side Pork

Stekt fläsk

1 lb. lightly salted or fresh
   side pork
1/2 cup milk

salt, optional
dash of pepper

Cut pork into slices as thin as possible. Remove rind or gash each
rind edge 2 or 3 times. Dip in milk if pork is very fat.
Place in hot skillet and fry until nicely brown on both sides. If fresh
pork is used, season with salt and pepper.
Serve with Onion Sauce, see below, and boiled potatoes in their
jackets, or with Brown Beans, Swedish style, p. 78, and spiced or fried
apple rings.
4 servings.

Onion Sauce

Löksås

1 cup chopped onion
1–2 tbsp. butter
2 tbsp. flour
2 cups milk

1 tsp. salt
dash of pepper
pinch of sugar

Sauté onion gently in butter in saucepan until tender. Sprinkle with
flour and add milk gradually while stirring. Simmer 5 min., stirring
occasionally. Season.
4 servings.

Öland Potato Dumplings

Öländska kroppkakor

Potato dumplings are oldtimers in the sturdy diet of the farm people.
There are many regional varieties, but the dumplings of the island of
Öland in the Baltic Sea have won acclaim over the others.

Dough:
3 medium raw potatoes
2 cups mashed potatoes
3/4 cup flour
3/4 cup barley flour
1 tsp. salt

Stuffing:
1/2 lb. salt side pork, cubed
2 tbsp. chopped onion
1 tsp. crushed allspice
To every qt. water:
1 tsp. salt

Peel and grate potatoes. Place in sieve and press out water. Mix
grated potatoes with other ingredients for dough until well blended.
Fry pork and onion. Add allspice.

Fried
Side Pork
and Brown
Beans

*Stekt fläsk
och
bruna bönor*

Preparing
Potato
Dumplings

Kroppkakor

Shape dough into long roll on floured board and cut into 10 slices. Flatten slices and make a depression in each. Fill with stuffing and press together like a bun, see picture. Buns should be round and without cracks. Cook in salted water $1/2$–$3/4$ hour. Serve immediately with melted butter and lingonberries.
4 servings.

Swedish Meatballs   *Köttbullar*

GROUND MEAT DISHES

Swedish Meatballs   *Köttbullar*

1 tbsp. butter
3 tbsp. chopped onion
$1/2$ cup bread crumbs
$11/4$ cups milk
$1/2$ lb. ground beef
$1/2$ lb. ground lean pork
1 egg
2 tsp. cornstarch
$11/2$ tsp. salt
$1/4$ tsp. pepper

To fry:
2–3 tbsp. butter
Gravy:
pan drippings
1 tbsp. flour
$3/4$–1 cup milk or water
salt and pepper

Melt butter in skillet and sauté onion golden brown. Soak bread crumbs in milk. Add meat, egg, onion, cornstarch, salt, and pepper and mix thoroughly until smooth. Shape into balls the size of a walnut, using one hand and a tablespoon dipped in cold water.

52

Brown butter in skillet and fry meatballs in batches of about 10–15 until evenly brown, shaking pan continuously to make balls round.
Remove each batch to hot saucepan and clean skillet with a little water before starting next, saving pan juice so obtained.
When all meatballs are fried, cook 2 min., in saucepan. Remove meatballs to hot serving platter, leaving pan drippings in saucepan.
Mix flour and milk and stir into pan juice. Simmer 5 min. Add more milk or cream, if too thick, and season.
Pour gravy over meatballs or serve separately.
Serve with boiled potatoes, or Browned Potatoes, recipe p. 76, or spaghetti, vegetables, Cucumber salad, recipe p. 75, and lingonberries.
4 servings.

Lindström's Hamburgers   *Biff à la Lindström*

1½ lb. ground beef

2 eggs

½ cup light cream and water

2 boiled medium potatoes, mashed

¾ cup chopped pickled beets

2 tbsp. chopped onion

2 tbsp. chopped capers

2 tbsp. liquid from pickled beets

½ tbsp. salt

¼ tsp. pepper or paprika

To fry:

3 tbsp. butter

½ cup water

Mix ground meat and potatoes. Add eggs and liquid gradually while stirring. Carefully mix in beets, onion and capers. Season. Shape into patties, ½ inch thick. Fry quickly in butter on both sides in skillet. Place on hot platter and garnish with parsley. Rinse skillet with water and pour drippings over patties.
Serve immediately with fried or boiled potatoes and vegetable salad.
6 servings.

Meat-Stuffed Onions   *Fylld lök*

10 medium yellow onions

half of stuffing as in recipe for Cabbage Rolls below

To braise:

2 tbsp. butter

¾ cup liquid in which onions are cooked

Continued next page.

Fylld lök

Peel onions and boil in slightly salted water 10 min. Drain. Remove centers of onions and fill with stuffing, see picture. Place a couple of onion leaves over each opening and tie with string. Heat butter in skillet and brown onions on all sides. Add stock, cover and simmer 20–30 min., or until done.
Serve as luncheon dish or on the Smörgåsbord.
4 servings.

Stuffed Cabbage Rolls   *Kåldolmar*

1 medium cabbage head	*To fry:*
Stuffing:	2 tbsp. butter
$1/2$ cup rice	1 tbsp. brown sugar or dark
1 cup water	corn syrup
1 cup milk	$1^1/2$ cups stock or water
$1/2$ lb. ground beef	*Gravy:*
$1/2$ lb. ground pork	pan drippings
1 egg	$1^1/2$ tbsp. flour
$1/2$ cup milk	$1/2$ to 1 cup milk or light cream
$1^1/2$ tsp. salt	salt, pepper
$1/4$ tsp. pepper	soy sauce, optional

54

Preparing
Stuffed Cabbage
Rolls

Kåldolmar

Cut out core of cabbage head and separate the leaves gently.
Place cabbage leaves in boiling, salted water (2 tsp. salt to every qt. water) and cook 5 min. Drain.
Rinse rice. Bring water to the boiling point, add rice and simmer until water is absorbed. Add milk and simmer until rice is tender (20 min.) stirring occasionally. Cool. Mix with ground meat, egg, milk, and seasonings. Trim thick center vein of each cabbage leaf. Place 2 tbsp. stuffing on each leaf. Fold leaf over stuffing, see picture, and fasten with toothpick or strings.
Heat butter in skillet and brown rolls on all sides. Place in Dutch oven or heavy kettle and sprinkle with brown sugar. Rinse skillet with a little boiling water and pour drippings over rolls. Add stock or water, cover and cook slowly 1 hour or until cabbage is tender, basting occasionally.
Arrange rolls in deep serving dish, removing toothpicks or strings. Mix flour and milk and stir into pan juice. Simmer 5 min., adding more milk if gravy gets too thick. Season and add soysauce. Pour gravy over rolls. Serve with boiled potatoes and lingonberries.
6 servings.

Swedish Hash   *Pytt i panna*

Swedish Hash   *Pytt i panna*

2 cups leftover meat, diced	3 tbsp. butter
2 cups boiled potatoes, diced	salt
1 medium onion, chopped	pepper

Melt part of butter in skillet and sauté onion until golden brown. Remove to plate. Brown potatos and then meat in remaining butter. Add onion and season. Arrange on hot platter and garnish with pickled cucumber and parsley. Serve with fried eggs and pickled beets or dill pickle.
4 servings.

Swedish Ways with Fish

With its long coastline and many lakes – 96,000 according to the statistics – as well as innumerable rivers, Sweden always leaned heavily on fish to provide its people with an adequate diet. In ancient times and until a few decades ago, the lowly salt herring was the chief source of protein and fat for the main part of the population. Even today, when modern refrigeration and freezing has made all kinds of seafood available the whole year around, even in places remote from the principal fishing waters, the salt herring in various preparations is highly favored. No Smörgåsbord deserves its name if it does not start with salt herring, home cured and industrially prepared in different ways. The most boiled-down version of the Smörgåsbord consists only of herring, cheese, and butter; *S.O.S. (Smör, Ost, Sill)*, as it is commonly abbreviated, is a standing item on the restaurant menu. But salt and cured herring are not only the most common everyday and party appetizers. Fried and served with onion sauce, herring is also a favorite main dish. Fresh fried herring with lingonberries enjoys the same popularity.

The first cousin of herring, the small-sized Baltic herring, *strömming*, is to be found on the east coast of Sweden. It is about the size of the sprat, smelt, or fresh sardine, which are good substitutes for the same ways of preparation. There are any number of Baltic herring dishes to choose from in its home region.

Cod, haddock, whiting, and other codfish, as well as many flounder varieties and mackerel, are highly popular everyday food. So are pike, pike-perch, and others among the fresh water fish. Dried cod has an old tradition in Sweden as in so many other countries of the world. It is often served in the form of pudding. The related dried ling-cod constitutes the Swedish Christmas fish, *lutfisk*, see p. 102. Salmon, trout, sole, and eel are the aristocrats on the table and preferred party food. It is particularly noteworthy that the eel belongs to this category. Most popular is smoked or jellied eel. Salmon is prepared through elaborate curing or smoking, as well as by plain poaching or sautéeing.

It is obvious that this high frequency in serving fish implies many delicious ways of preparing it. The recipes selected here represent some of them, such as poaching, baking, stewing, sautéing, curing, au gratin, pudding style, etc. A luscious sauce is often served to enhance the flavor of the fish or to give an interesting contrast, such as lemon sauce, Dutch sauce, horseradish sauce, sweet-sour sauce, etc. Shellfish, too, is served with great versatility, for examples see color picture, facing p. 24.

No less than three types of seafood are traditionally honored with special parties when in season. The gayest of them all is the crayfish party in August, the month of beautiful moonlight.

Every fall Baltic herring is enjoyed in its fermented stage in the northeast and northern parts of the country at special celebrations, and the eel, presented in manifold versions, is the target of special "eel banquets" in southern Sweden. Only one meat product is bestowed the same honor – the goose at Michaelmass time, which bears witness to the superior rank of fish to Swedish palates.

POACHED FISH DISHES

Poached Fish Fillets
with Lemon Sauce
Fiskfiléer med citronsås

2 lb. fillets of flounder, cod, or
haddock, fresh or frozen
1 tsp. salt
Stock:
2 cups water
1 cup dry white wine, optional
1 small carrot

2 slices yellow onion
1/2 bay leaf
3 parsley or dill sprigs
2 whole allspice
4 peppercorns
1 tbsp. butter

58

Poached Fish Fillets with Lemon Sauce   *Fiskfiléer med citronsås*

Roll fillets tight, fasten with toothpicks, and place close together in kettle.

Mix all ingredients for stock. Simmer 15 min. Strain and pour hot over fish. Simmer covered until fish turns white, 8–10 min. Length of cooking time depends upon kind of fish.

Remove fillets carefully onto hot platter.

Prepare Lemon Sauce, see recipe below, and pour over. Garnish with lemon slices, lettuce, tomatoes, shrimp, or dill sprigs. Serve with boiled potatoes.

Variation: Omit stock. Mix juice of half lemon with 2–3 tbsp. water, pour over fish and dot with 1 tbsp. butter. Simmer as above.
4 servings.

Lemon Sauce for Poached Fish Fillets   *Citronsås*

$1^1/_2$ tbsp. butter	salt, pepper
$2^1/_2$ tbsp. flour	juice of half lemon
$1/_2$ cup cream or milk	1 egg yolk
1 cup fish stock	2 tbsp. cream

Melt butter, stir in flour. Gradually add cream and fish stock, stirring constantly. Simmer 5 min. Remove from heat. Season and add lemon juice to taste. Beat egg yolk and cream together and stir into sauce.
4 servings.

Poached Pike with Horseradish Sauce

Kokt gädda med pepparrotssås

2 to 2¹/₂ lb. pike
1 tbsp. salt
¹/₂ tsp. vinegar
2 small carrots
1 leek
10 parsley sprigs

10 peppercorns
1 bay leaf
2 tbsp. butter
To boil:
2 cups hot water

Clean pike, rinse and drain. Rub with salt and vinegar, mixed together. Place fish on large sheet of aluminum foil with carrots, leek, parsley, peppercorn, and bay leaf. Dot with butter. Wrap well. Place in large baking pan, add water and cook in very hot oven (450°F.) 30–45 min. Serve with boiled potatoes and Horseradish Sauce, see recipe below. 4–6 servings.

Horseradish Sauce for Fish

Pepparrotssås till fisk

2 tbsp. butter
2¹/₂ tbsp. flour
1 cup milk
1 cup fish stock

salt, pepper
3 tbsp. grated horseradish

Melt butter in saucepan. Stir in flour, add liquid gradually and simmer 5 min., stirring occasionally. Season. Add grated horseradish. Do not boil sauce after adding horseradish or taste will be bitter. 4–6 servings.

Poached Salmon

Kokt lax

2 lb. cut of salmon
salt
Stock:
1 qt. water
3 tbsp. white vinegar
1 tbsp. salt
5 peppercorns
3 whole allspice

1 bay leaf
1 onion
1 carrot
about 10 dill sprigs
Garnish:
lemon slices, dill sprigs, or
   parsley

60

Clean fish. Sprinkle with salt.

Combine all stock ingredients and boil, covered, 15 min. Place fish and dill in boiling stock. Bring uncovered to boiling point and skim. Cover and simmer fish, 15–20 min.

Remove carefully onto platter. Garnish with dill sprigs or parsley and lemon slices. Serve hot with Dutch Sauce, see recipe below, and boiled potatoes.

Poached salmon may also be served cold as Smörgåsbord dish. Chill fish in strained stock. Garnish with tomatoes and cucumber. Serve with freshly grated horseradish and sour cream or with mayonnaise.

Eel, mackerel, or *trout* may be substituted for salmon. Cooking time 10–12 min.

4–6 servings.

Dutch Sauce

(Hollandaise Sauce)   *Hollandässås*

4 egg yolks	2 tbsp. lemon juice
3 tbsp. hot water	salt, pepper
1/2 cup butter	

Beat egg yolks and water in double boiler over hot water for 1 min. Melt butter. Pour into egg mixture, season, stirring until thick. Add lemon juice to taste. Serve immediately or, if not served directly, keep uncovered. Delicious sauce for all kinds of boiled or poached fish.

4–6 servings.

OVEN DISHES WITH FISH

Baked Fish Fillets with   *Ugnstekta fiskfiléer*
Dill and Tomatoes   *med tomat och dill*

2 lb. fillets of haddock, cod, or mackerel, fresh or frozen	1 big bunch of dill (20–25 sprigs) or 2 tbsp. dried or frozen dill
2 tsp. salt	
4 tomatoes, sliced	3 tbsp. butter

Sprinkle fillets with salt. Place in buttered baking dish. Sprinkle with chopped dill and put tomatoes on top. Dot with butter. Bake in very hot oven (450°F.) 10–15 min.

Serve with boiled or mashed potatoes.

4–6 servings.

Baked Eel   *Ugnstekt ål*

1 eel (about 2 lb.)   3 tbsp. bread crumbs
$1/_2$ tbsp. salt   salt, pepper
juice of half lemon   *To bake:*
Coating: 2 tbsp. butter
1 egg

Loosen skin around neck of fish and draw it off with a piece of cloth
in hand. Remove head. Split fish open and clean thoroughly. Remove
backbone, being careful not to pierce meat. Drain on absorbent paper.
Rub eel with salt and lemon juice. Brush with beaten egg. Mix bread
crumbs, salt, and pepper and sprinkle over fish. Place eel in buttered
baking dish and bake in very hot oven (450°F.) 30–40 min. Baste
frequently and add hot water if needed.
Serve hot or cold with boiled potatoes, salad, and Sweet-Sour Sauce,
see recipe below.
4 servings.

Sweet-Sour Sauce for Fish   *Skarpsås*

1 yolk from hard-boiled egg   dash of white pepper
1 raw egg yolk $1^1/_2$ tsp. sugar
$1^1/_2$ tbsp. lemon juice $3/_4$ cup heavy cream
$1/_2$ tsp. mustard
$1/_4$ tsp. salt

Pass cooked egg yolk through sieve and mix with raw egg yolk and
lemon juice. Add seasonings. Fold in whipped cream very carefully
and serve immediately. If sauce shows sign of curdling, add small
amount of heavy cream and stir until smooth.

Stewed Lake Perch   *Stuvad abborre*

8 lake perch (about 2 lb.)   3 tbsp. chopped parsley
$1^1/_2$ tsp. salt   2 tbsp. chopped chives
dash of pepper   2 tbsp. flour
3 tbsp. butter   1 cup water

Scale and clean fish. Sprinkle with salt and pepper. Place fish close
together in greased baking dish, sprinkle with parsley and chives. Mix

Stewed Perch   *Stuvad abborre*

flour and water and pour over fish. Dot with butter. Cover and simmer in hot oven (450°F.) 15–20 min. Serve from baking dish with boiled potatoes.
4 servings.

Baked Whitefish   *Ugnstekt sik*

2 to 2¹/₂ lb. whitefish	1 tsp. salt
1 tbsp. salt	*To fry:*
Coating:	3 tbsp. butter
1 egg	¹/₂ cup water
3 tbsp. bread crumbs	¹/₂ cup light cream

Scale and clean fish, removing gills but not head. Rinse and drain. Rub with salt. Brush with beaten egg, turn in bread crumbs and salt. Place in buttered baking pan and dot with remaining butter. Bake in very hot oven (475°F.) 20–30 min. Baste frequently with butter and after 10 min. with hot water and cream. When done, fish should flake easily from bones but still be moist. Serve from baking dish garnished with parsley and lemon slices, with boiled potatoes and vegetables.

Cod, haddock, salmon, or pike may be substituted for whitefish.
4–6 servings.

Wrapping Stuffed Fish before Baking   *Fisk i kapprock*

Creamed Fish in Casserole   *Stuvade fiskfiléer i form*

$1^1/_2$ lb. fillets of cod or   1 piece of root celery, cubed
    haddock, fresh or frozen   1 carrot, sliced
$1^1/_2$ tsp. salt   2 tomatoes, sliced
$^1/_2$ tsp. white vinegar   dash of pepper
2 tbsp. butter   1 tbsp. flour
1 leek, sliced   1 cup cream or milk

Mix salt and vinegar and rub into fillets. Heat 1 tbsp. butter and sauté leek, celery, and carrot. Do not brown. Layer fillets, tomatoes, and fried vegetables in greased casserole. Sprinkle between layers with pepper. Mix flour and milk until smooth and pour over Dot with remaining butter. Cover and bake in hot oven (425°F.) 20–30 min. 4 servings.

Baked Stuffed Fish in Foil   *Fisk i kapprock*

4 mackerel, herring, or trout $^1/_2$ cup chopped parsley
    (about 2 lb.) $^1/_4$ cup chopped dill sprigs
2 tsp. salt $^1/_4$ cup chopped chives
Stuffing: $^1/_4$ cup chopped onion
2 tbsp. butter   2 tbsp. lemon juice

Garnish: parsley, lemon slices

Cut open back of fish and remove bones and entrails. See picture. Rinse and drain. Sprinkle with salt.

Mix stuffing and pack into fish. Wrap each fish individually in aluminum foil or buttered wax paper, see picture. Fold ends of paper. Bake in hot oven (400°F.) 20 min. Remove to hot platter and garnish with parsley and lemon slices. Serve in jackets with boiled or mashed potatoes and lettuce salad.

4 servings.

Lobster au Gratin   *Gratinerad hummer*

2 boiled lobsters, split   3 tbsp. grated Parmesan cheese
3 tbsp. butter   salt
1 tbsp. flour   dash of cayenne pepper
1 cup cream   *Garnish:*
2 egg yolks   dill sprigs or chopped parsley

Remove lobster meat and cube. Clean shells and save.

Melt butter, add flour and stir until well blended. Gradually stir in cream. Cover and simmer 5 min., stirring occasionally. Remove from heat. Add egg yolks and 1 tbsp. grated cheese. Heat, stirring, but do not boil. Season.

Remove from heat. Stir constantly until thick. Add lobster meat, stirring carefully.

Fill shells with mixture. Sprinkle with grated cheese. Place under broiler or in extremely hot oven (500°F.) 5 min. until golden brown. Garnish with dill sprigs or chopped parsley and serve immediately.

4 servings.

Fish au Gratin   *Fiskgratäng*

2 lb. fillets of sole, flounder,   1¹/₂ cups fish stock and light
   or pike, fresh or frozen   cream
salt, pepper   2 egg yolks
3 tbsp. lemon juice   3 tbsp. cold butter
1 tbsp. butter   salt, pepper
Sauce: 2 tbsp. grated cheese
2 tbsp. butter   *Garnish:*
1 tbsp. flour   4¹/₂-oz. can shrimp or mussels

Fiskgratäng

Sprinkle fillets with salt and pepper. Place in buttered baking dish, pour lemon juice over, dot with butter. Cover with aluminum foil and bake in hot oven (425°F.) 10 min.

Prepare sauce. Melt butter in saucepan, stir in flour. Add cream and fish stock gradually while stirring and simmer 5 min. Remove from heat and stir in egg yolks and cold butter. Heat but do not boil, stirring constantly. Season. Remove from heat.

Garnish fish with shrimp or mussels. Pour sauce over. Force Mashed Potato, see recipe below, through pastry tube along edge of fish platter. Sprinkle with grated cheese. Place under broiler or in extremely hot oven, (500°F.) and bake for 10 min. or until golden brown.

6 servings.

Mashed Potato for Fish au Gratin   *Potatismos Duchesse*

1 lb. potatoes (3 medium	2 egg yolks
potatoes)	1/4 cup milk
water, salt	salt, pepper
1 tbsp. butter	

Peel potatoes and boil in salted water until soft. Drain. Mash thoroughly. Add butter, milk, and egg yolks and beat until light and fluffy. Season.

4 servings.

Sautéed Fish

*Stekta
fiskfiléer*

SAUTÉED FISH DISHES

Sautéed Fish   *Stekta fiskfiléer*

8–10 fish fillets (about 2 lb.)   *To fry:*
1^1/$_2$ tsp. salt   3 tbsp. butter
juice of half lemon   *Garnish:*
Coating: lemon, parsley
1 slightly beaten egg
bread crumbs

Rinse and drain fish fillets. Sprinkle with salt. Dip in egg, then in
bread crumbs. Let coating stiffen a few minutes.
Melt butter in skillet and sauté fish on both sides until golden brown.
Remove to hot platter. Mix lemon juice into pan drippings and pour
over fish. Garnish with lemon and parsley. Serve with boiled potatoes,
salad, and butter mixed with chopped parsley.

Fried Salt Herring   *Stekt salt sill*

2 salt herring   3 tbsp. butter
bread crumbs or rye flour ^{1}/$_2$ cup cream
2 onions, sliced

Continued next page.

Fillet herring and soak overnight in cold water in cool place, preferably refrigerator. Remove small bones and skin. Drain on absorbent paper. Turn fillets in bread crumbs.

Heat butter and sauté onion until soft. Remove onion and fry fillets golden brown on both sides. Pour cream over and simmer 1 min. Remove fillets to hot platter and pour over gravy and onion.

Serve with boiled potatoes in jackets or baked potatoes.

Onion and cream may be omitted and dish served with Onion Sauce, see recipe, p. 50.

4 servings.

Fried Stuffed Smelts or Sardines *Strömmingsflundror*

2 lb. smelts, sardines (fresh, not canned) or small herring
$^1/_2$ tbsp. salt

Stuffing:
2 tbsp. butter
$^1/_2$ cup chopped parsley, dill and chives

Coating:
1 egg, optional
bread crumbs or rye flour or whole wheat flour

To fry:
$^1/_4$ cup oil or butter

Clean fish. Remove heads, tails, entrails, and bones. Rinse. Drain on absorbent paper. Spread out skin-side down and sprinkle with salt. Mix butter and herbs and spread stuffing on half number of fishes. Cover with remaining fishes. Coat with beaten egg, then bread crumbs, see picture.

Preparing Stuffed Smelts or Sardines *Strömmingsflundror*

Fry in fat in skillet until golden brown and serve hot with mashed potatoes, lingonberries, and Cucumber Salad, recipe p. 75.
Leftovers are delicious marinated, see recipe below.
4 servings.

Marinated Fried Sardines or Smelts *Inlagd stekt strömming*

2 lb. fried sardines or smelts (see recipe above)

Dressing:

1 cup white vinegar

$1/2$ cup sugar

7 peppercorns

6 whole allspice

2 bay leaves

1 red onion, sliced

dill sprigs

Garnish:

1 red onion

dill sprigs

Combine all ingredients for dressing. Mix well and let stand 10 min. Pour over warm fish. Refrigerate overnight. Garnish with fresh dill sprigs and onion rings. Serve as luncheon dish or with Smörgåsbord.
6 servings.

FISH PUDDINGS AND MOLDS

Herring Pudding *Sillpudding*

1 salt herring (about $1/2$ lb.)

4 medium potatoes, boiled

2 onions, sliced

pepper

3 eggs

1 tsp. flour

2 cups milk

Fillet herring. Soak overnight in cold water. Drain fillets and cut in even slices, about 1″ thick. Peel potatoes and cut in thin slices.
Layer potatoes, herring, and onion in buttered baking dish, with potatoes in bottom and on top. Sprinkle between layers with pepper.
Beat eggs, flour and milk together and pour over pudding.
Bake in hot oven (400°F.) 30 min., or until golden brown. Serve in baking dish with melted butter.
4 servings.

Salmon Pudding *Laxpudding*

One-half pound cured salmon can be substituted for herring in recipe above. Use chopped parsley in place of onions.

Codfish Pudding
Kabeljopudding

1 lb. raw (or 2 cups cooked)	3 tbsp. bread crumbs
salt dried cod	3 tbsp. butter
2/3 cup rice	2 eggs
1 1/3 cups water	salt, optional
3 cups milk	pepper

Soak fish overnight in cold water. Cook, chill, bone, and cut in small pieces.
Rinse rice under hot running water. Bring water to the boiling point, add rice and simmer until water is absorbed. Add milk gradually and bring to boil, cover and simmer 30 min. or until rice is tender, stirring occasionally.
Mix rice with butter, fish and eggs. Season and pour into greased and breaded baking dish. Sprinkle with bread crumbs and dot with butter. Bake in hot oven (400°F.) 30 min. Serve with melted butter.
Leftovers may be sliced and fried in butter. 4 servings.

Fish Soufflé
Fisksufflé

1/4 cup butter	1 1/4 tsp. salt
1/3 cup flour	1/4 tsp. pepper
1 1/2 cups milk	*For casserole:*
4 eggs	butter
2 cups boiled fish, cut in pieces	bread crumbs

Melt butter and stir in flour until well blended. Add milk, stirring, and cook 3–4 min. Remove from heat and add egg yolks, one by one, stirring vigorously. Add fish and season. Remove from heat, stir until slightly cooled.
Fold in stiffly beaten egg whites. Pour mixture into well greased and breaded baking dish. Bake in slow oven (325° F.) until set, about 45 min.
Serve immediately in baking dish with Lobster Sauce, recipe below, Mushroom Sauce, recipe p. 39, or melted butter. 4 servings.

Lobster Sauce
Hummersås

2 tbsp. butter	1 cup light cream
2 tbsp. flour	1 boiled lobster or one 5-oz.
1 cup milk and lobster stock	can lobster meat
from can	salt, pepper

70

Fish in Aspic

Fisk i gelé

Melt butter, add flour and stir until well blended. Add stock, milk and cream gradually, stirring constantly. Simmer 5 min., stirring occasionally. Add lobster meat, cut in pieces and season. Heat but do not boil. Serve with boiled fish, boiled vegetables, fish puddings, soufflés, etc.
4 servings.

Fish in Aspic   *Fisk i gelé*

2 to 2¹/₂ lb. salmon, mackerel
   or eel
Stock:
To every qt. water:
1 tbsp. white vinegar
1 tbsp. salt
5 peppercorns
5 whole allspice
1 bay leaf
plenty of dill, optional

Aspic:
4 cups strained fish stock
2 envelopes unflavored gelatin
¹/₂ cup cold water
2 egg whites, slightly beaten
salt, pepper
Garnish:
shrimp, eggs, tomatoes

Mix all ingredients for stock and simmer 15 min.
Clean fish and cut in about 1″ slices. Simmer in stock about 10 min. Let fish cool in stock.

Aspic: Remove fish from stock. Skim off fat. Soak gelatin in cold water for 10 min. Bring cold fish stock, egg whites and gelatin slowly to the boiling point. Remove from heat and let stand 15 min. Skim and strain. Season. *Continued next page.*

71

Cover bottom of mold with small amount of aspic. Chill until set. Arrange on top of aspic, shrimp and sections of eggs and tomatoes in attractive pattern. Pour over small amount of aspic. Refrigerate until set. Arrange cold fish on top and pour over remaining aspic. Chill until set. Unmold and serve with mayonnaise as Smörgåsbord or luncheon dish.
6 servings.

CURED FISH

Salt Herring with
Sour Cream Dressing *Salt sill med grädde*

Fillet herring and soak 2–3 hours in cold water, in cool place, preferably refrigerator. Remove small bones and skin. Rinse and drain. Cut in slices, $1/2''$ thick. Slide spatula under slices and arrange on dish. Sprinkle with chopped chives or garnish with dill sprigs.
Serve as main dish or appetizer, chilled, with sour cream, mixed with chopped chives, and new potatoes boiled with dill.

Smoked Salmon
Served Swedish Style *Rökt lax på svenskt vis*

Arrange slices of smoked salmon on platter. Garnish with lettuce leaves and dill sprigs. Serve with poached eggs, buttered spinach and boiled new potatoes. Or serve as appetizer with dill sprigs and lemon sections.

How to Serve Fermented Baltic Herring *Surströmming*

Fermented Baltic Herring is a specialty of North Sweden, highly cherished by most people in that part of the country. It is in season in the early fall when special "Surströmming" parties are given. It has a penetrating odor, repugnant to those who are not used to it, though many gradually acquire a taste for the dish and even become fans. It is sometimes available in Swedish delicatessen stores in the U.S.
The fish is served directly from the can or arranged on a serving dish. When served from can, open $1/2$ hour before serving time to allow odor to "steam off" partially. If arranged on serving dish, rinse herring in soda water, drain and keep in cool place until serving time.
Serve with finely chopped onion, boiled potatoes, thin crisp bread *(Tunnbröd)*, butter and goat cheese.

Dill-Cured Salmon
Gravlax

3 to 4 lb.-cut of salmon	*Dressing:*
dill sprigs	3 tbsp. olive or salad oil
$2/3$ cup salt	$1^1/_2$ tsp. vinegar
$1/2$ cup sugar	$1/2$ tsp. French mustard
20 white peppercorns, crushed	$1/4$ tsp. salt
pinch of saltpeter, optional	dash of white pepper
(available in drug stores)	sugar, optional

Select middle cut of 6 to 7 lb.-salmon. Remove bone and cut in two pieces lengthwise. Rinse and dry on absorbent paper. Mix salt, sugar and pepper and – to retain red color of salmon – pinch of saltpeter. Rub part of seasonings into fish.

Place thick layer of dill sprigs in bottom of pan or bowl. Place one piece of salmon, skin-side down, in pan and sprinkle with remaining seasonings and cover with plenty of dill sprigs. Put other piece of fish on top, skin-side up. Cover with board and put weight on top. Keep in refrigerator 16–24 hours.

Remove spices and cut salmon into slices. Arrange on platter and garnish with dill sprigs and lemon slices. Shake together all ingredients for dressing and let stand 5 min. before serving. Serve with dressing, buttered spinach and boiled potatoes, or as appetizer. 8 servings.

Cooked Crayfish
Kokning av kräftor

The catching of crayfish in lakes and rivers is allowed from midnight between August 7 and 8 until the end of September. The first crayfish parties take place on the evening of August 8. They are gay affairs. Weather permitting, they are held outdoors. Colored paper lanterns illuminate the garden, and, if one is lucky, they are outshone by the August moon.

40 crayfish	5 tbsp. salt
4 qt. water	dill crowns and sprigs

It is very important that every crayfish is alive when put into boiling water. Rinse live crayfish in cold water.

Boil water, salt and dill 2–3 min. Remove dill.

Plunge half of crayfish into rapidly boiling water. Cover and bring again to boil. Add remaining crayfish, cover and bring to boil. Add more dill. Boil 7–9 min. Cool in stock and refrigerate before serving. Arrange crayfish on platter and garnish with plenty of dill crowns.

Serve with toast and butter. Various kinds of cheese, coffee and cake may follow.

Vegetable Dishes
—a Few Still Popular Oldtimers

The growing season is short in the northern parts of the world. Fresh vegetables had a limited spell in bygone days, but were avidly enjoyed when at their peak in summer. The remaining part of the year they necessarily played a minor role. Today this picture has changed entirely. Improved growing methods, importation, canning, and freezing have made them increasingly available. They are prepared and served much the same way as in other countries. Until fairly recently potato and rutabaga (in England called turnip) were the principal all-year-round vegetables. Dried peas and beans provided important variation during the long winter. A basic vegetable since long ago times is the green cabbage. Root crops like carrot and parsnip were also stored for winter use. Some old ways of presenting these provisions, like Brown Beans Swedish Style, Yellow Pea Soup, Lamb in Cabbage, Mashed Rutabaga, Potato Griddle Cakes, and Dumplings still have an established reputation for their culinary merit. You will find them among the recipes in this book as well as cucumber and beets, marinated in vinegar, both still highly cherished relishes with meat and fish dishes.

There are from 40 to 50 varieties known of edible mushrooms growing in the Swedish forests. Like the Finns, Russians, Poles, and some other nationalities, Swedish housewives make great use of these gifts of nature. Mushroom picking is a favorite pastime of many people, young and old. Their harvest is brought home and proudly served sautéed or creamed, separately, or in combination with other foods.

Cucumber Salad   *Inlagd gurka*

1 medium cucumber $^1/_2$ tsp. salt
1 cup white vinegar   dash of pepper
$^1/_2$ cup sugar   2 tbsp. chopped parsley

Peel cucumber and slice thinly. Place in bowl. Mix remaining ingredients, except parsley. Let stand 10 minutes and pour over cucumber.
Sprinkle with parsley. Refrigerate about 3 hours. Serve with fried
meat or poultry.

Pickled Beets   *Inlagda rödbetor*

20 small beets   *Dressing:*
1 qt. water   1 cup vinegar
2 tsp. salt $^1/_4$ cup water
                                  $^1/_2$ cup sugar
                                  1 clove

Place whole beets in salted, boiling water and boil 20–40 min. or until
tender. Drain, peel, cool and cut in thin slices. Place in glass dish.
Mix all ingredients for dressing and pour over. Leave in refrigerator
1–3 hours before serving.

Onion Casserole   *Löklåda*

2 tbsp. butter $^3/_4$ cup cream
1 lb. small onions, sliced   1 tsp. salt
$^1/_2$ lb. ground pork $^1/_4$ tsp. pepper
$^1/_2$ lb. ground veal $^1/_2$–$^3/_4$ cup vegetable or
$^1/_3$ cup bread crumbs   beef stock
$^3/_4$ cup water

Melt butter in skillet and sauté onion until golden brown.
Soak bread crumbs in water, add meat and season. Mix thoroughly
until smooth, adding cream gradually.
Cover bottom of buttered casserole with half amount of onion, spread
meat on top and cover with remaining onion. Pour some stock over,
making holes in mixture to let stock through.
Bake in moderate oven (375°F.) 30–40 min. Cover if top becomes
too brown. Serve very hot as Smörgåsbord dish or luncheon dish.
6 servings.

Potato Griddle Cakes   *Raggmunkar, Rårakor*

8 medium potatoes   1 tsp. sugar
1 egg   1 tsp. salt
3 tbsp. flour   *To fry:*
1/2 cup milk   butter or bacon fat

Mix all ingredients, except potatoes, until smooth. Wash, peel and
grate potatoes. Add to batter. Heat griddle or frying pan, grease and
cover bottom with thin layer of batter. Brown on both sides and turn
onto hot platter. Proceed in the same way with remaining batter. Serve
immediately with fried salt pork and lingonberries or apple sauce.
4 servings.

Potato Salad   *Potatissallad*

6 cold, boiled medium potatoes,   *Dressing:*
    sliced   2 tbsp. wine vinegar
2 tbsp. chopped onion   6 tbsp. olive or salad oil
2 tbsp. chopped parsley   1 tsp. salt
2 tbsp. chopped chives or 2 tbsp.   1/4 tsp. pepper
    chopped capers, optional
1/2 cup diced, pickled beets

Shake all ingredients for dressing. Arrange potato slices in salad bowl
with onion, parsley, chives, capers, and beets in rows on top. Pour
dressing over. Refrigerate 1–2 hours.
Turn once or twice just before serving. Serve with sausages, pigs'
feet or cold meat.
4 servings.

Browned Potatoes   *Brynt potatis*

10 medium potatoes, boiled in   1/2 cup bread crumbs
    jackets   1 tsp. salt
3 tbsp. butter   dash of pepper

Peel potatoes and shape into small balls. Brown half of butter in
skillet. Add half of potatoes, and sprinkle with half of bread crumbs.
Season and shake continuously until potatoes are covered with crumbs
and nicely brown. Remove from pan and proceed in same way with
remaining potatoes. Serve with fried meat or fish. 8 servings.

76

Potato Griddle Cakes with Lingonberries   *Raggmunkar med lingon*

Brown Beans, Swedish Style *Bruna bönor*

Swedish brown beans are available in Scandinavian delicatessens. They come closest to kidney beans among American varieties.

1²/₃ cups dried, Swedish brown beans	1¹/₂ tsp. salt
	2¹/₂ tbsp. dark corn syrup
5 cups water	3 tbsp. white vinegar

Wash beans and soak overnight in salted water. Bring to boil quickly and then cook slowly, covered until tender, 1¹/₂—2 hours. Add more water if necessary. Season to taste with salt, syrup and vinegar. Serve with Fried Side Pork, or Swedish Meatballs.
4 servings.

Mashed Rutabaga *Rotmos*

Rutabaga is the old peasant name for this vegetable in the southern part of Sweden. Through Swedish immigrants, it has also become known under this name in the U.S. In England it is called turnip.

1 medium rutabaga (1 lb.)	5 allspice
4 medium potatoes (1 lb.)	salt, optional
3–4 cups pork stock or water	pepper
5 pepper corns	

Peel rutabaga and potatoes and cut into large cubes. Cook rutabaga with seasonings in stock or slightly salted water 15 min., add potatoes and cook until soft. Drain, mash and gradually add small amount of stock. Season. Beat until smooth. Serve with slightly salted rib of beef or leg of pork or with Boiled Pork Sausage, see recipe p. 101.
4 servings.

Sautéed Mushrooms *Stekt svamp*

1 lb. mushrooms	salt, pepper
3 tbsp. butter	1 tsp. lemon juice

Clean mushrooms and slice lengthwise. Brown butter in skillet, add mushrooms and sauté over low heat until soft and golden brown. Season and add lemon juice. Serve on Smörgåsbord or with meat or fish dishes.
4 servings.

78

Dessert Favorites

Sweden is located within the same latitudes as Alaska. This means that only a limited range of fruits and berries can grow there. Among the wild ones, lingonberries, blueberries, blackberries, and raspberries are the most important. The polar circle crosses the northern part of the country which is favored by a couple of wild specialties: cloudberry, which is shaped like a raspberry but yellow in color, and the delicious arctic raspberry. Cloudberries are also encountered on bogs and marshes in other parts of the country. It is honored with the name "The orange of the North", due to its high content of ascorbic acid, exceeding that of the orange. The wild small-fruited strawberry, *smultron,* is quite common in the central and southern parts of the country. Rose hips from the wild rose bush are also used. Gooseberry, raspberry, strawberry, red and black currant, apples, pears, and plums are cultivated varieties. Chiefly due to the long days of light in the growing season of these northern areas, berries and fruits, both wild and cultivated, are of superior flavor and texture. Nutritionwise, they have a particularly high content of vitamin C.

In the old days, these choice products were stored away for the winter season through drying and other similar preserving methods; later by making fruit syrups, jams, and jellies. They traditionally form the bases for desserts the whole year through. Hence the dominance of fruit and berry stews, soups, and junkets as dessert dishes. They are also eaten with Swedish pancakes, waffles, and puddings which are generally served to make a meal with soup as the main course, more substantial. Dried rose hips are made into a rich, traditional soup, very common all year round and an excellent source of ascorbic acid. Blueberry soup is another favorite.

In summer the exquisite fresh berries served "au naturel" with milk or cream were, and are, the main dessert treat. A worthy rival is chilled, set clabbered milk, the so called *filbunke*, served with sugar, cinnamon, ginger, and gingerbread cookies.

Apple being the principal local fruit, is a great asset for the home-maker from the beginning of the Fall all through winter. It consti-tutes a real challenge to her gastronomic imagination and is pre-pared in many intriguing ways, of which only a limited few are handpicked for this recipe collection. Apple cake and other apple desserts are often accompanied by vanilla sauce, and so are baked fruit desserts like pies and the like. Vanilla sauce in this connection takes the place of ice cream in the American manner of serving pies and puddings "à la mode". Apple sauce is extremely common as a dessert, often prepared in the homes together with lingon-berries.

For party occasions ice cream served in fancy ways, parfaits, Bavarian creams, mousses, and the like lend festivity to the menu. Today oranges and other citrus fruits, peaches, bananas, pineapple, grapes, etc. are brought in from various countries in large quan-tities. Canned and frozen items of these, as well as of the local fruits and berries, are on hand in great variety. Many homemakers, in addition to canning, also make their own frozen preserves from home-grown products. This has brought many changes to the dessert habits.

Many of Europe's famous dessert-type cheeses are nowadays pro-duced in excellent quality within the country; others are imported, and they are becoming increasingly popular. A beautifully arranged tray with an assortment of cheeses, grapes or other fruit, radishes, and various types of crackers and bread, served with red wine, is looked upon as fit for any festive occasion.

Fruit Juice
Pudding

Saftkräm

FRUIT PUDDINGS AND SOUPS

Fruit Juice Pudding   *Saftkräm*

$1^1/_2$ cups fruit or berry juice   sugar to taste
$2^1/_2$ cups water   3 tbsp. cornstarch

Bring juice, water, and sugar to boil. Mix cornstarch with small
amount cold water. Remove saucepan from heat. Stir cornstarch into
syrup and bring again to boiling point. Simmer 3 min., stirring occasionally. Remove to serving bowl.
Cover and cool. Serve with cream or milk.
4 servings.

Fruit Soup   *Fruktsoppa*

1 package mixed, dried fruit   1 cinnamon stick, optional
  (12 oz.)   grated rind of half lemon
6 cups water   2 tbsp. tapioca
$1/_2$ cup sugar   juice of half lemon

Mix all ingredients except lemon juice and cook slowly, covered, until
fruit is tender, 30–40 min. Chill. Add lemon juice. Serve with rusks.
6 servings.

Rhubarb Pudding   *Rabarberkräm*

1 lb. rhubarb (4–5 stalks)	1 cup sugar
1 cup water	2 tbsp. cornstarch

Cut rhubarb in pieces. Bring water to boil, add rhubarb and sugar, and boil until rhubarb is almost tender.
Mix cornstarch with small amount of cold water. Remove saucepan from heat. Stir in cornstarch, simmer for 3 min. Remove to serving bowl, cover and cool. Serve with cream or milk.
4 servings.

Blueberries, strawberries, raspberries, and other berries can be substituted for rhubarb. Take sugar to taste.

Gooseberry Pudding   *Krusbärskräm*

1 qt. unripe gooseberries	1 cup sugar
1 1/2 cups water	2 tbsp. cornstarch

Trim and rinse gooseberries.
Bring water and sugar to the boiling point. Add gooseberries and simmer 5 min.
Mix cornstarch with small amount of water. Remove saucepan from heat, stir in cornstarch. Bring again to boil and simmer 3 min.
Remove pudding to bowl, cover and chill.
Serve with light cream or milk and Almond Rusks, recipe p. 131.
4 servings.

Rose Hip Soup   *Nyponsoppa*

In Scandinavia the ripe, red hips of wild roses are used in dried form for dessert dishes like soup, junket, and sauce, to which they lend a delightful, unique flavor. In addition, they have a very high vitamin C content. Instant dried rose hip mix is sometimes sold in Scandinavian delicatessen stores.

2 cups dried rose hips (1/2 lb.)	*Garnish :*
1 1/2 qt. water	slivered almonds
1/2 cup sugar	light or whipped cream
1 1/2 tbsp. cornstarch	

Crush rose hips. Bring water to boil, add rose hips. Cover and cook 45 min., stirring occasionally. Strain through sieve. Measure liquid and return to saucepan. Add enough water to make 1 1/2 qt. liquid.

Clabbered
milk with
Ginger Snaps

*Filbunke med
pepparkakor*

Mix cornstarch with small amount of water. Add cornstarch and sugar
to soup. Heat and simmer 3 min. Cover and chill.
Garnish with slivered almond and a spoonful or two of whipped cream
for each serving or some light cream. Serve with Almond Rusks,
recipe p. 131.
4 servings.

Clabbered Milk   *Filbunke*

Set sour milk or cream, *filbunke,* is a refreshing summer treat, highly
popular in Sweden. Excellent filbunke is served as a meal starter in
many good restaurants.
Smear bottom of 4 individual glass or china bowls with 1/2 tbsp. sour
cream. Put in warm place and fill up with milk. For best result, use
fresh whole milk containing no preservative. Cover and leave until
milk has set. Chill.
Serve with sugar, ginger or cinnamon, Swedish crisp bread or ginger
snaps, see picture.

APPLE DESSERTS

Almond Apple Cake   *Mandeläpplekaka*

2 cups apple slices, fresh or   1/2 cup sugar
   canned (No. 303 can)   2/3 cup blanched, ground
3 eggs   almonds

Continued next page.

If fresh apples are used, boil slices with $1/4$ cup water and $1/2$ cup sugar for 5 min.

Drain apple slices. Spread evenly in buttered baking dish. Beat eggs and sugar until white and fluffy. Add almonds.

Pour egg mixture over apples. Bake in moderate oven (350°F.) 30–40 min. Serve cold with cream or Vanilla Sauce, recipe p. 86.

6 servings.

Stuffed Baked Apples   *Fyllda stekta äpplen*

See color picture, facing p. 48.

8 sour apples	2 tbsp. water
Stuffing:	*Coating:*
$1/2$ cup ground, blanched almonds	$1^1/2$ tbsp. melted butter
	$1/2$ cup sifted bread crumbs
$1/4$ cup sugar	2 tbsp. sugar

Mix almonds with sugar and water until smooth. Peel and core apples. Fill centers with almond paste.

Roll apples in melted butter, then in bread crumbs mixed with sugar. Bake in buttered baking dish in hot oven (425°F.) about 25 min. or until apples are soft and nicely brown. Serve from baking dish with whipped cream or Vanilla Sauce, recipe p. 86.

8 servings.

Baked Apple Dumplings   *Äppleknyten*

See color picture, facing p. 48.

8 sour apples	*Stuffing:*
Pastry:	3 tbsp. sugar
1 cup cold, unsalted butter	1 tsp. cinnamon
1 tbsp. sugar	2 tbsp. butter
2 cups pastry flour	*Topping:*
$1/4$ cup ice water	1 tbsp. sugar
	$1/4$ cup chopped almonds or nuts

Sift flour onto baking board. Mix with sugar. Cut butter into flour mixture with pastry blender. Gradually add ice water and mix into dough. Handle dough as little as possible. Chill for 30 min. or more. Roll out dough into a rectangle, about $1/4''$ thick. Fold two times and roll out again. Chill. Repeat this procedure twice. Chill.

Peel and core apples.

Apple
Dumplings
ready for the
oven

Äppleknyten

Roll out dough and cut into 5″ squares. Place an apple in center of each square. Fill center of apples with stuffing. Fold corners of pastry over apple, pinching edges together, see picture. Brush with beaten egg, sprinkle with sugar and almonds.
Bake in hot oven (400°F.) 30–40 min. or until apples are soft and pastry nicely brown.
Serve hot or cold with whipped cream or Vanilla Sauce, see recipe p. 86. 8 servings.

Apple Cake with Vanilla Sauce   *Äpplekaka med vaniljsås*

This delicious apple cake is sometimes called Danish, sometimes Swedish. It is actually highly popular all over Scandinavia.

$^1/_4$ cup butter
$1^1/_2$ cups fine breadcrumbs

2 cups apple sauce (no. 303 can)

Melt butter in skillet, add bread crumbs and sauté until nicely brown, stirring constantly.
Layer bread crumbs and apple sauce in buttered baking dish, three layers bread crumbs and two layers apple sauce. Bottom, medium and top layers should be bread crumbs. Dot with remaining butter and bake in hot oven (400°F.) for 30 min.
Cool and unmold. Garnish with powered sugar, see picture, p. 86. Serve with Vanilla Sauce, see p. 86.
4 servings.

Swedish Apple Cake with Vanilla Sauce   *Äpplekaka med vaniljsås*

Vanilla Sauce for Apple Desserts   *Vaniljsås*

3 egg yolks   2 tsp. vanilla extract
2 tbsp. sugar   1 cup whipped cream, optional
1 cup light cream

Beat egg yolks and sugar in top of double boiler. Heat cream, add to mixture and simmer until thick, stirring constantly. Remove from heat. Let cool, beating occasionally. Add vanilla extract. When cold, gently fold in whipped cream and serve.
4 servings.

PANCAKES, WAFFLES, PUDDINGS

Swedish Pancakes   *Plättar*

In every Swedish home you find a *plättpanna*, i.e. a special frying pan used only for these small, thin pancakes, about 3 inches across. Served with sugar and jam, they are a favorite treat among both children and adults, and constitute the standard dessert following the Yellow Pea Soup on the classical Thursday dinner menu, see picture p. 28.

1 cup flour	3 eggs
2 tbsp. sugar	3 cups milk
1/4 tsp. salt	2 tbsp. melted butter

Sift flour into bowl. Add sugar and salt. Stir in eggs and milk gradually until smooth. Add butter. Heat Swedish pancake pan (or regular pancake pan) and butter well. Pour batter by tablespoonfuls into sections of pan and fry on both sides until nicely brown. Place on hot platter and serve immediately with lingonberries or other jam.
4 servings.

Variation: Pancakes may be fried in 7" frying pan and then folded and heated before serving in chafing dish in butter, flavored with orange juice and grated orange rind, see color picture, facing p. 48.

Poor Knights   *Fattiga Riddare*
(French Toast)

12 slices stale coffee bread or	1 tbsp. sugar
white bread	1 tsp. cinnamon
Batter:	2 cups milk
1/3 cup flour	2 eggs
1/4 tsp. salt	

Sift flour into bowl. Add sugar, salt, and cinnamon. Stir in eggs and milk gradually until smooth. Dip bread slices in mixture.
Heat butter in skillet. Brown slices on both sides. Serve very hot with jam or lingonberries.
4 servings.

Rice Pudding   *Risgrynskaka*

Prepare Rice Porridge, see recipe for Christmas Porridge, p. 103. Remove from heat and cool slightly.
Stir in 2 eggs, slightly beaten, and 1/2 cup raisins. Flavor with grated rind of lemon, or shredded almond, or vanilla. Pour into well greased and breaded baking dish. Bake in hot oven (400°F.) 45 min. Serve hot or cold from baking dish with Fruit Juice Sauce, recipe p. 88.
Slice leftovers and sauté in butter.
6 servings.

Fruit Juice Sauce for Puddings   *Saftsås*

1/2 cup sweetened fruit juice   1/2 cup water
  (raspberry, strawberry or   juice of half lemon
  other berry)   11/2 tsp. cornstarch

Mix all ingredients. Heat. Simmer 3 min., stirring occasionally. Cover
and cool. Serve with dessert puddings. 4 servings.

Dessert Waffles   *Frasvåfflor*

As the picture shows, Swedish waffles are heart-shaped. This type of
waffle iron is sometimes available in Scandinavian specialty stores and
gift shops.

13/4 cups heavy cream   1 tbsp. sugar
11/2 cups cake flour   3 tbsp. melted butter
1/2 cup ice water   1/2 tsp. salt

Beat cream until stiff. Sift in flour, add ice water, sugar and salt and
stir until well blended. Pour in melted butter.
Heat waffle iron slowly. Brush generously with butter. Pour in batter
by tablespoonfuls and bake until golden brown. Place waffles on rack
to keep crisp. Serve immediately with coffee or as dessert with jam and
sugar and whipped cream.
Makes about 8 waffles.

Rennet Pudding   *Kalvdans*
See color picture, facing p. 48.

11/2 qt. rennet   1/2 tsp. salt
  (about third day)   10 ground, blanched almonds or
1 egg, optional   1 tsp. cinnamon
1 tbsp. sugar

Mix all ingredients.
Try out batter by pouring 1/2 cup into small bowl. Place bowl in slowly
boiling water and simmer until custard forms. (If not set by 15 min., add
1 egg to batter. If too stiff, add small amount of regular milk. Try out
batter again. Add more egg or milk, if needed.)
Fill batter into greased baking dish. Cover and place in water-filled
pan. Bake in moderate oven (375°F.) until set, 30–45 min. or less.
Serve hot or cold with jam or lingonberries. If desired, chill and slice
and sauté slices lightly in butter. 6 servings.

Dessert Waffles   *Frasvåfflor*

SOME PARTY DESSERTS

Lemon Bavarian Cream   *Citronfromage*

2 eggs	1/4 cup water
1/2 cup sugar	1 cup heavy cream
3 tbsp. lemon juice	*Garnish:*
grated rind of 1/2 lemon	slivered almonds and blue
1 envelope unflavored gelatin	grapes

Beat egg yolks and sugar until white and fluffy. Add lemon juice and
rind. Soften gelatin in 1/4 cup cold water and dissolve over low heat
until liquid. Stir into egg mixture.
Place in refrigerator until thick but not set. Stir occasionally.
Fold in stiffly beaten egg whites and whipped cream.
Rinse 5-cup mold in cold water. Pour mixture into mold. Keep in
refrigerator 3 hours or until set.
Unmold. (If difficult, dip mold an instant in hot water.) Garnish with
grapes and slivered almond and serve with fancy cookies.
4–6 servings.

Pineapple
Bavarian
Cream

*Ananas-
fromage*

Pineapple Bavarian Cream   *Ananasfromage*

1 envelope unflavored gelatin
$1/4$ cup cold water
2 eggs
$1/2$ cup sugar
juice of half lemon
$1/2$ cup pineapple juice
1 cup heavy cream, whipped
1 cup pineapple chunks, drained
(No. 211 can)

Soften gelatin for 5 min. in $1/4$ cup cold water.
Beat egg yolks and sugar until smooth. Add lemon and $1/2$ cup pineapple juice. Dissolve gelatin over low heat until liquid. Add to egg mixture and refrigerate until thick, but not set.
Gently fold in stiffly beaten egg whites, cream, and well drained pineapple chunks.
Rinse a 5 cup mold in cold water. Pour mixture into mold. Place in refrigerator for 3 hours or until set. Unmold. (If difficult, dip mold an instant in hot water.) Garnish with pineapple slices and cherries.
4–6 servings.

Strawberry Parfait
Jordgubbsparfait

1¹/₂ cups crushed strawberries
¹/₂ cup sugar
¹/₄ cup water

2 egg yolks
1 cup heavy cream

Simmer sugar and water for 5 min.
Beat egg yolks in top of double boiler, adding sirup gradually. Simmer over hot, not boiling water, until mixture thickens. Remove from heat and stir occasionally until cold.
Add 1 cup crushed strawberries and fold in whipped cream. Pour into low mold and freeze until firm (3–5 hours or more).
Remove to refrigerator 15 min. before serving time. Unmold onto serving platter. (If difficult, dip mold an instant in hot water.) Slice, if desired, and garnish with remaining ¹/₂ cup strawberries. Serve with fancy cookies.

Raspberries may be substituted for strawberries.
4 servings.

Note: Frozen strawberries (1 lb. package) may be substituted for fresh strawberries. Then omit sugar and water and add ¹/₂ cup of juice from frozen berries.

Caramel Custard
Brylépudding

For mold:
1 cup sugar
3 tbsp. boiling water
For custard:
4 eggs
1¹/₂ tbsp. sugar

1 tbsp. vanilla or grated rind
   of half lemon
1 cup milk
1²/₃ cups light cream
Garnish:
15 blanched almonds

Melt sugar in skillet over low heat until brown syrup forms. Stir occasionally with wooden spoon until all lumps are gone. Add boiling water and stir until mixture is transformed into syrup. Coat bottom and sides of warm ring mold or baking dish with syrup.
Beat eggs, sugar, vanilla, milk and cream in bowl. Pour mixture into syrup-coated mold. Place deep, oblong baking pan in oven and fill with hot water. Place mold in the water and bake in slow oven (300°F.) 45 min. or until custard is set. Chill and unmold on serving platter, garnish with almonds and serve with syrup as sauce.
4 servings.

*Strutar med
fyllning*

Cornucopias

Strutar med fyllning

2 eggs
$3/4$ cup sugar
$3/4$ cup flour
2 tbsp. melted butter
Filling:
1 cup heavy cream
1 tbsp. sugar, optional
1 cup jam or fresh or frozen
    berries, crushed

Beat eggs and sugar until white and fluffy. Add sifted flour and stir until well blended. Add butter.

Grease and flour cookie sheets. Trace circles on sheets using a saucer as a guide.

Spoon 2 tbsp. batter in centre of each circle and flatten out with spatula, dipped in cold water. Cookies should measure about 6″ across. Bake in moderate oven (375°F.) until golden brown, about 4 min.

Remove cookies immediately one at a time and shape into cones. (If cookies become brittle, warm quickly in oven.) Stack cones in a glass to keep them in shape.

Fill immediately before serving with whipped cream, mixed with berries, mashed with a little sugar, or with jam, see picture.

Makes about 20 cones.

Orange Chocolate
Pudding

Chokladpudding

Orange Chocolate Pudding   *Chokladpudding*

1 envelope unflavored gelatin
$^1/_4$ cup water
1 egg, separated
$^1/_2$ cup sugar
$^1/_4$ cup cocoa
$^1/_2$ cup light cream
3 tbsp. frozen orange juice
   concentrate
1 cup heavy cream
2 tbsp. candied, chopped orange
   peel, optional

Garnish:
green grapes or candied orange
   peel, whipped cream

Soften gelatin in cold water.
Mix egg yolk, sugar, cocoa, and light cream in top of double boiler
and cook until thick, stirring constantly.
Remove from heat. Add gelatin and juice and allow to cool, stirring
occasionally until mixture starts thickening.
Beat egg white until stiff. Fold into mixture together with whipped
cream. Add chopped candied orange peel, if desired.
Rinse mold in cold water. Pour mixture into mold. Chill 2–3 hours
or until set.
Unmold. (If difficult, dip mold an instant in hot water.) Garnish and
serve with fancy cookies.
6 servings.

Merry Christmas
in Sweden
— Some Traditional Treats

Christmas in Sweden is, like everywhere else, a time both for religious worshipping and secular rejoicing. But in the Scandinavian countries Christmas was always observed very intensively because of their northern location, which means that darkness and winter storms prevail during this period.

Christmas commemorates the birth of Christ, but long before the country was christened in the ninth century, a big midwinter feast was held by the Vikings to celebrate the winter solstice and the return of light. Along with elaborate rites to move their gods into arranging the return of the sun, the revival of nature, and an abundant crop during the coming growing season, went a happy revelling in food and drink. This tradition has never been abolished.

THE "YULE PIG" – JULGRISEN – AND OTHER MEAT FARE

On the farms in olden times the Christmas preparations started early in November with the slaughtering of those animals which should not or could not be fed during the winter season. The meat was preserved by the primitive methods of these ages, such as salting, the making of sausages, smoking, etc. Special Christmas sausages and brawns, such as Head Cheese and others, were made, and the finest ham, spareribs and pig's head were reserved for Christmas. The daily diet of the people was often frugal during this period and almost always lacked variation, no fresh vegetables, fruits or fish being available. The new grain crop was not yet being converted into flour, and the meat supply was scarce until the cold came, which made slaughtering and storing possible. The raw climate required sturdy fare, and everybody longed for Christmas and the lavish diet, especially of pork dishes. Even today, these

94

dishes are traditional at Christmas, although life is so much easier all year round that they are not really required. On the contrary, the Christmas diet nowadays is almost too rich and filling. Sausages, brawns, etc. are in most cases now bought ready made, although many homemakers, especially farm women, still prepare their own from old recipes handed down through generations. If you wish to try them, you find recipes for some of these old favorites on the following pages.

LUTFISK

Pork was already the main treat during heathen times at the midwinter festival. The Catholic church introduced a Lenten period before Christmas which required a fish diet. The only fish available was dried fish (Ling, a codfish variety) which was lime-cured, a process which had to be started on December 6, if the fish should get ready in time. Even today – in spite of the fact that the Swedish people is almost one hundred per cent Lutheran, and no Lenten food restrictions are prescribed – *lutfisk* (Lye fish) is traditional Christmas fare. Most people, however, buy it cured and ready for the kettle. It is generally available in Scandinavian specialty shops at Christmas time. On page 102 you find a recipe for the baking of lutfisk and directions for its serving.

CHRISTMAS BREADS AND COOKIES

One thing which is still the joy of most homemakers is the baking of all kinds of traditional buns, cookies, and cakes, although these are available in the bakeries in satisfactory and, in some cases, excellent quality. The Christmas buns and other saffron breads as well as some of the cookies, especially the gingerbread varieties, differ in shape from the all-year-round ones. They are all traditional and have special names like Christmas Wagon, Vicar's Hair, Church Entrance, Golden Wheel, Sun Wheel, etc. The gingerbread cookies are shaped like animals, stars, human beings, etc. Many of them have a mythological background and were meant to symbolize and promote the fertility of the soil during the coming year. On the color picture facing page 113, you will find an assortment of these Christmas Breads and Cookies, for which recipes are given in the baking chapter. The gingerbread house on the color picture facing p. 112 constitutes a delightful Christmas table centerpiece. The children, from the toddler stage upwards, share in the joy of Christmas baking and they also delight in preparing – with mother's help – some of their own Christmas "goodies", such as Almond Toffee and Chocolate Toffee, for which recipes are given here.

DIPPING DAY

Just like children in any country, Swedish children, stirred up by all the preparations going on, become impatient and often ask their mothers when Christmas Eve will come. In Sweden that is the day they get their gifts, so no wonder they want to know. Mother might answer them: "Today is the day before the day before the dipping day – *Dopparedagen*." It is an old custom, still in use in almost every family, to have a large kettle of hot stock from the boiling of Christmas ham and other pork on the stove for the early dinner of Christmas Eve. Into this pot everyone dips one or more slices of a special kind of bread baked with stout and called *Vörtbröd*. That is why Christmas Eve has the popular name of "Dipping Day". The bread is eaten with ham, spareribs, and sausages. For dessert various kinds of jam and cookies, preferably Christmas crullers, are served.

Late in the evening after various kinds of Christmas celebrations have taken place – a visit to the church for the Christmas Eve service, the distribution of Christmas gifts at home, etc. – a big supper follows with all the Christmas fare on the table, arranged like the Christmas Smörgåsbord you see in the color picture between pages 24 and 25. The meal ends with rice porridge and milk. In the porridge is one blanched almond, and the one who gets the almond, if he or she is an unmarried, fairly grown-up person, is said to marry during the coming year! The *Jultomten* – Santa Claus – should have his portion of porridge, too.

The happy mixture of pagan and Christian celebrations which constitutes the Swedish Christmas is clearly reflected in the traditional foods of the season. The recipes and pictures here give you a chance to share in its many delights.

96

Christmas Ham

Home Cured Christmas Ham   *Julskinka*

10 lb. fresh ham
1 cup salt
$1/4$ cup sugar
$1^1/_2$ tsp. saltpeter (available in
   drug stores)
Brine:
To every qt. water:
$1/_2$ cup salt
1 tbsp. sugar
1 tsp. saltpeter

To cook:
water
1–2 bay leaves
10 white peppercorns and
   allspice
Glaze:
1 egg white
1 tbsp. mustard or mustard
   powder
1 tbsp. sugar
bread crumbs
Garnish:
kale or parsley

Rub ham with mixture of salt, sugar, and saltpeter and place in large container or stone crock. Keep in cool place 3 days, turning ham occasionally. *Continued next page.*

97

Make brine of boiling water, salt, sugar, and saltpeter. Cool and pour over ham. Brine should cover ham. Weigh down with board and leave in cool place 10 days, turning occasionally.

Remove ham, wipe well and place with fat side up in enough boiling water to cover. Bring water to the boiling point again and skim. Add bay leaves and pepper. Cover and simmer very slowly 3–4 hours or until tender. Remove skin and all loose fat from ham. Let cool overnight in stock in cool place.

Beat egg white, mix with mustard and sugar. Spread evenly on ham and sprinkle with bread crumbs. Bake in very hot oven (475°F.) 10 min.

Strain stock, season and use for "Dip in the Kettle", see p. 96. Cover knuckle of ham with red and white paper frill and decorate ham with creamed butter using fine pastry tube, see picture, p. 97. Place on large platter and garnish with kale or parsley.

Head Cheese *Pressylta*

See color picture between pages 24 and 25.

4 lb. lean pork	1/2 bay leaf
2–21/2 lb. veal shoulder	2–3 onion slices
1 large piece hog's rind	1/2 carrot
For boiling:	*Spices:*
To every qt. water:	2 tbsp. salt
1 tbsp. salt	2 tsp. pepper
5 whole allspice	1/4 tsp. allspice
5 white peppercorns	1/4 tsp. cloves
1–2 cloves	

Place meats and rind in boiling water to cover. Bring water to the boiling point, skim, and add remaining ingredients for boiling. Simmer 11/2–2 hours or until tender. Do not boil too long, as head cheese then gets a brittle texture. Remove meat. Save stock.

When cold, cut all meat into thin slices. Spread cloth or towel wrung out in hot water in deep bowl, and line with rind, right side down. Arrange fat and lean meat in alternate layers, sprinkling spices on each layer. Cover with pieces of rind. Pull cloth together tightly and tie securely with string.

Place head cheese in saucepan, cover with stock and cook slowly 10 min. Remove to platter, cover with weighted board.

Remove cloth after 24 hours. Keep head cheese in strongly salted water. Serve sliced with pickled beets.

98

Jellied Veal

Kalvsylta

Jellied Veal   *Kalvsylta*

See color picture between pages 24 and 25.

2 lb. veal shank	2 bay leaves
2 lb. lean side pork	6 cloves
1¹/₂ qts. water	1 onion
2 tbsp. salt	1 carrot
15 white peppercorns	pepper to taste
10 whole allspice	2 tbsp. white vinegar

Place meat in large kettle and barely cover with cold water. Bring water to the boiling point. Skim. Add seasonings, onion, and carrot. Simmer 1¹/₂–2 hours or until meat is tender.

Remove meat and when cold, cut in small cubes or put through grinder. Return bones to stock and simmer 30 min.

Strain stock, return to kettle, add meat, and bring to the boiling point. Season with pepper and vinegar.

Pour mixture into molds, rinsed in cold water and chill until set. Unmold on serving dish, cut in slices and serve with pickled beets.

Liver Paté Loaf   *Leverpastej*

See color picture between pages 24 and 25.

1 lb. veal or beef liver	3 eggs
¹/₂ lb. fresh, fat pork	1¹/₃ cups cream
¹/₂ cup chopped onion	1 tbsp. salt
8 Swedish anchovy fillets	¹/₂ tsp. pepper
(Marinated sprats in can)	*For mold:*
¹/₄ cup flour	²/₃ lb. fat pork cut in thin slices

Continued next page.

99

Wash liver and soak 15 min. Rinse and dry. Remove membranes and tubes. Cut liver and fat pork in pieces and grind together with onion and anchovies 3 to 4 times. Force through sieve.

Beat eggs, cream, and flour until well blended and add gradually to liver mixture, stirring vigorously. Add seasonings and continue to beat until well blended. Line loaf pan with thin slices of fat pork, fill $3/4$ full with liver mixture and cover with aluminum foil.

Place deep, oblong baking pan in oven and fill with hot water. Place loaf pan in the water and bake in slow oven (325°F.) $1^1/_2$–$1^3/_4$ hours. Keep in mold until cold or until following day.

Unmold and serve sliced with cucumbers and tomatoes, bread and butter.

Browned Red Cabbage   *Brynt rödkål*

2 small heads red cabbage, shredded or cubed

3 tbsp. butter

2 tbsp. dark corn syrup

2 apples, peeled and sliced

1 onion, grated

juice of one lemon

$1/_3$ cup vinegar or red wine

1 tsp. salt

Melt butter in heavy skillet. Add cabbage and syrup and brown over slow fire, stirring constantly. Add apples, onion, lemon juice, vinegar, and salt. Simmer covered 1–$1^1/_2$ hours, stirring occasionally. Season to taste. Serve with roast goose or ham.

8–10 servings.

Christmas Pork Sausage   *Fläskkorv*

3 lb. lean pork shoulder

1 lb. boneless veal

1 lb. fat pork

$3/_4$ cup potato flour or 1 lb. potatoes, about half-baked

$3/_4$–1 qt. water or half water and half beef or pork stock

$2^1/_4$ tbsp. salt

1 tbsp. sugar

$1^1/_4$ tsp. pepper

$1^1/_4$ tsp. allspice

$3/_4$ tsp. ginger

About 4 yards casing

Curing:

2 tbsp. salt

2 tbsp. sugar

1 tsp. saltpeter (available in drugstore)

Ask your butcher to grind all meat except fat pork 2 times, add fat pork and grind 2 times more. Mix all ingredients, except liquid, in large bowl and work by hand for one hour, adding liquid a little at a time. Check seasoning by boiling a small ball of batter in saucepan.

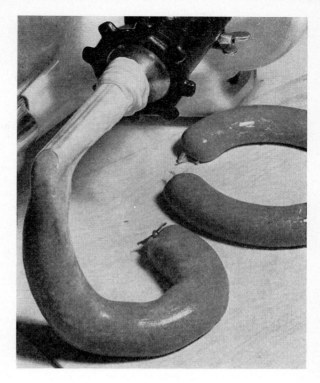

Fläskkorv

Mixture should have the consistency of a porous but fairly thick porridge. If too thin, add some extra cornstarch.

Cut casings into 15″ lengths and tie each at one end. Fill loosely, see picture, and tie other end. Rinse sausages in cold running water and drain on towel. Rub with curing mixture and keep in refrigerator overnight. Rinse. The sausage can be kept in refrigerator for a few days. If to be kept several weeks, place in cold cooked brine (for recipe see Christmas Ham, p. 97.

Makes 7 lb.

Boiled Pork Sausage   *Kokt fläskkorv*

2 lb. pork sausage, recipe above.

Place sausage in saucepan and cover with cold water. Heat slowly, reduce heat just before boiling point is reached and simmer 30 min. Remove to hot platter, cut in slices and serve with mashed potatoes, or Mashed Rutabaga, recipe, p. 78, and mustard. 4 servings.

Liver and Rice Pudding

Korvkaka

2 lb. veal or beef liver
1 cup rice
2 cups water
1 qt. milk
$1/4$ lb. pork

1 onion
$1/2$ cup seedless raisins
2 tbsp. dark corn syrup
2 tsp. salt
$1/4$ tsp. pepper

Soak liver about 15 min. in cold water. Rinse rice. Bring water to boiling point, add rice and simmer until water is absorbed. Add milk and bring again to boiling point. Cover and simmer until rice is tender (45 min.), stirring occasionally.
Grind liver, pork and onion. Rinse raisins in hot water. Mix all ingredients and season. Pour mixture into well buttered and breaded baking dish and bake in moderate oven (350° F.) for 1 hour. Serve hot with lingonberries and melted butter. 6 servings.
Slice leftovers, fry in butter and serve with lingonberries.

Baked Lutfish

Lutfisk kokt i ugn

Lutfisk (lye-fish) is the Swedish Christmas fish. It is spring-ling, a cod-fish variety, which is lime-cured. Earlier, this was made in the homes; today lutfish is mostly bought ready for cooking. It is available in Scandinavian delicatessen stores at Christmas time.

3 lb. lutfish (ready to cook)   1 tbsp. salt
1 tbsp. butter

Place lutfish, skin-side down, on buttered baking dish. Sprinkle with salt. Cover with aluminum foil and bake in moderate oven (350°F.) 30–40 min. Baking time depends upon how thick fish is. Pour off water before serving. Remove foil and serve with White Sauce, see recipe below, salt, pepper and mustard.
4 servings.

White Sauce for Lutfish

Vitsås

3 tbsp. butter
2 tbsp. flour
$2^1/_2$ cups milk or half milk
    and half cream

1 egg yolk
salt, pepper

Baked Lutfish   *Kokt lutfisk*

Melt butter, stir in flour and gradually add milk. Simmer 5 min.,
stirring occasionally. Season. Remove from heat. Add slightly beaten
egg yolk.
4 servings.

Christmas Rice Porridge   *Risgrynsgröt*

1 cup rice	1 stick cinnamon
1 tbsp. butter	1 tsp. salt
1 cup water	2 tbsp. sugar
5 cups milk	

Rinse rice. Melt half of butter in saucepan or double boiler, add
rice and water and boil 10–15 min. or until water is absorbed. Add
milk and cinnamon stick and simmer 45 min. or until milk is almost
absorbed, season and add remaining butter. Serve with cold milk,
cinnamon and sugar.
6 servings.

Almond Toffee *Knäck*

1 cup sugar
1 cup dark corn syrup
1 cup heavy cream

1 cup blanched almonds,
  coarsely chopped
1/4 cup butter

Mix sugar, syrup and cream in skillet. Cook over low heat, stirring constantly, until a few drops of mixture dropped into cold water can be shaped into a soft ball (250°F. on the candy thermometer). Add almonds and butter and spoon up mixture into small fluted paper candy cups, see picture, or onto buttered cookie sheet 10″×15″. Allow to set. While cooling, mark squares with oiled knife. Break into pieces when cold.
Makes about 60 candies.

Chocolate Toffee *Chokladkola*

2 3/4 cups sugar
1 1/4 cups dark corn syrup
1/4 cup cocoa

3 tbsp. butter
2 1/4 cups cream
1 tbsp. vanilla extract

Mix all ingredients and cook over slow heat, stirring occasionally, until a few drops of mixture dropped into cold water, can be shaped into a soft ball (250°F. on the candy thermometer). Pour into well-buttered 9″×9″ cake pan. Cool slightly and cut in small squares with oiled knife. Wrap in waxed paper.

Christmas Glögg *Julglögg*

Glögg means glow and derives its name from the burning of the sugar over the drink. It is the common Swedish Christmas punch bowl. Nowadays glögg is often served less strong, made exclusively on dry red wine, aquavite being omitted. Ready-mixed glögg spices are sold in Scandinavian delicatessen stores.

1 bottle Swedish aquavite
  (brännvin)
1 bottle Claret, Burgundy
  or other dry red wine
10 cardamom seeds
5 whole cloves

3 pieces of dried orange peel
4 dried figs
1 cup blanched almonds
1 cup raisins
1 1/2 inch cinnamon stick
1/2 lb. sugar cubes

Pour spirits into kettle. Add remaining ingredients except sugar cubes, cover and heat slowly to boiling point. Remove from heat.

Almond
Toffee

Knäck

Chocolate
Toffee

- *Chokladkola*

Put sugar in sieve with long handle. Dip into hot liquid to moisten.
Light sugar with a match and allow to burn. Continue dipping sieve
into liquid until sugar has melted into glögg. Cover kettle to put out
flame. Cool. Keep in closed bottles.

Heat glögg before serving, but do not boil. Serve hot in wine glasses
with a few raisins and almonds in each glass.

Breads Pastries
Cakes and Cookies

To throw a coffee party is the simplest and the most common form of entertaining in Sweden. Still a coffee party is quite an elaborate affair by U.S. standards. Traditionally there should be a minimum of seven varieties of breads, pastries, cookies, and cakes: the prelude being a rich coffee bread as a solid foundation for the more delicate things that follow, i.e., plain cake such as Sunday Cake, Chocolate Cake, Ginger Cake, Jelly Roll or similar items. Ginger snaps and three to four types of minor cookies come next, and finally a succulent, decorated cake or torte. In earlier days, this was all homemade, and baking was the pride and joy of every homemaker.

Today there is a marked tendency to pare down on this, but there are seldom less than four or five varieties. An increasing number of homemakers resort to buying most of their baked goods in the many bakeries and other stores, where they are available in good, even excellent quality. Cake mixes are also gaining ground.

In most homes, though, a weekly Sunday Cake, *sockerkaka,* is prepared. Especially at Christmas, many homemakers go out of their way in order to please family and friends with homemade traditional types of bread and cookies. The coffee bread then is flavored with saffron, and cookies are made in special shapes as told on page 95 where the special Christmas fare is described.

The bakeries have long since taken over the greatest part of ordinary bread-baking, such as the favorite *limpa* and other rye bread varieties, and the making of hardtack bread, *knäckebröd,* has been completely industrialized.

On the color pictures facing pages 49 and 113, as well as in the black and white pictures in this section, you will find most of the old favorites like vanilla rocks, polynées, *sandbakelser,* rosettes, and many others which are still common and cherished delicacies. The recipes enable you to make them all with the genuine Swedish slant.

106

RYE BREAD

Swedish Limpa   *Limpa*

1 package active dry yeast

$1/4$ cup water

$1/4$ cup lard or butter

1 cup milk (skim milk or regular)

$1/4$ cup dark corn syrup

$3/4$ tsp. salt

$1^1/2$ tsp. fennel or anise seed, pounded

3 cups rye flour (in Swedish *rågsikt)*

$1^1/4$ cup all-purpose flour

Dissolve yeast in warm water (110°F.).
Melt fat, add milk and cool until lukewarm. Pour into big bowl, add syrup, salt, seeds, yeast mixture and half of rye flour. Mix well. Add remaining rye flour. Gradually work in all-purpose flour, saving about $3/4$ cup. Beat well until dough is smooth and firm. Cover with towel and let rise in warm place until almost double in bulk. Work in about half of remaining all-purpose flour.
Turn dough into floured board and knead well. Divide in 2 equal portions. Shape into loaves. Place on greased baking sheet. Cover and let rise in warm place until double in bulk (about 1 hour).
Bake in hot oven (400°F.) about 30 min. Remove to rack, brush with warm water, cover with towel and let cool. Makes 2 loaves.

Flat Rye Bread   *Hålkakor*

Prepare dough as in recipe above for Swedish Limpa.
Divide dough in 2 equal portions. Shape into round flat loaves about size of medium dinner plates. Cut out a small round hole in center. Place on greased baking sheet, prick with fork, cover and let rise 45 min.
Bake in hot oven (425°F.) 15–20 min. until light brown. Remove to rack, brush with warm water and cover with towel.
Makes 2 loaves.

Rye Bread Loaf   *Formbröd*

Prepare dough as for Swedish Limpa, see recipe above.
Turn dough onto floured baking board. Shape into one loaf and place in greased loaf pan. Prick with fork. Cover and let rise until double in bulk (about 1 hour). Bake in slow oven (325°F.) 45–60 min. or until toothpich comes out clean. Unmold, brush with warm water, wrap in big towel, and let cool. Makes 1 loaf.

COFFEE BREADS

Coffee Bread   *Vetebröd*

2 packages active dry yeast
$1/4$ cup water
$1/2$ cup butter
$3/4$ cup milk
$1/2$ tsp. salt
$1/2$ cup sugar
1 egg ($3/4$ for dough, $1/4$ for brushing)

15 cardamon seeds, crushed, or $11/2$ tsp. pulverized cardamom, optional
$31/2$-4 cups flour (bread and pastry flour or all-purpose flour)

Dissolve yeast in $1/4$ cup warm water (110°F.).
Melt butter in saucepan and add milk. Chill until lukewarm.
Mix all ingredients with half of flour, preferably with wooden spoon, until dough is smooth and elastic, adding more flour gradually. Save about 1 cup flour.
Sprinkle dough with small amount of flour. Cover with clean towel and let rise in warm place until double in bulk (50–60 min.). Punch

Coffee Bread   *Vetebröd*

Preparing Cinnamon Ring

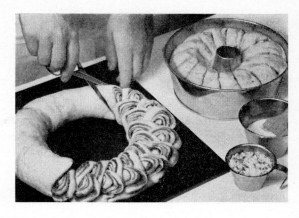

Kanelkrans

down dough and turn onto lightly floured baking board and knead until smooth, adding small amount of flour gradually, if necessary. Shape dough into desired shapes, see below.

Yield: 1 Cinnamon Ring
  or 2 Coffee Braids
  or 2 doz. Cinnamon Buns

Note: This coffee bread keeps very well for a few days if stored the proper way at room temperature in covered metal box with tiny air hole. It can be refreshed, just before serving, by being heated in very hot oven (450°F.) until soft, about 5 min.

Cinnamon Ring   *Kanelkrans*

Prepare dough as for Coffee Bread, see recipe above.
Roll out dough on floured baking board into 24″×10″ square. Spread thin layer of softened butter over dough. Sprinkle with sugar and cinnamon. Roll up dough jelly roll fashion. Pinch ends together. Remove ring to buttered baking sheet. Cut ring with scissors, see picture. Cover and let rise until almost double in bulk (about 1 hour). Brush with slightly beaten egg. Sprinkle with chopped almond and sugar. Brake in moderate oven (375°F.) 25–30 min. Cover and let cool on rack.

Coffee Braids   *Veteflätor*

Prepare dough as for Coffee Bread, see recipe above.
Divide dough into two parts to make 2 braids. Cut each portion into 3 equal parts. Shape parts into strands, 12″ long. Braid. Place on greased baking sheet. Cover and let rise until double (about 45 min.). Brush with beaten egg. Sprinkle with sugar. Bake in moderate oven (375°F.) about 20 min. Cover and let cool on rack. Makes 2 braids.

109

Cinnamon Buns

Kanelbullar

Cinnamon Buns　　　　　　　　　　　　　　*Kanelbullar*

Prepare dough as for Coffee Bread, see recipe p. 108.
Roll out dough on floured baking board into 24″×10″ square. Spread
thin layer of soft butter over dough. Sprinkle with sugar and cinnamon.
Roll up dough jelly roll fashion. Cut roll into 1″ slices. Place on
greased baking sheet. Cover and let rise until double in bulk (about
30 min.). Brush with beaten egg. Bake in very hot oven (475°F.) 8–10
min. Remove from baking sheet. Cover and cool on rack.
Makes 2 doz. buns.

Saffron Bread　　　　　　　　　　　　　　*Saffransbröd*

1 package active dry yeast	$1/_4$ tsp. salt
$1/_4$ cup water	$1/_2$ cup chopped raisins
$1/_2$ cup butter	2 eggs
$3/_4$ cup milk	4 cups flour (bread and pastry
1 tsp. saffron	flour or all-purpose flour)
$1/_2$ cup sugar	

Dissolve yeast in warm water (110°F.).
Melt butter in saucepan, add milk and let cool until lukewarm. Dry
saffron a few minutes on a piece of aluminum foil in very slow oven
(250°F.). Crush with 1 tsp. sugar and dissolve in a few tablespoons
of milk.
Mix all ingredients in bowl with half of sifted flour. Beat with wooden
spoon until very smooth and shiny. Add flour gradually. The dough
should be quite light. Save about 1 cup flour. Sprinkle small amount

of flour over dough and cover with towel. Let rise until double in bulk, about 1 hour.

Add about $1/4$ cup flour more and work dough until it does not stick to bowl.

Turn dough onto floured baking board and shape into braids or Lucia Buns, see below and color picture facing p. 113.

Makes 2 braids or $1^1/_2$–2 doz. Lucia buns.

Saffron Braids   *Saffransflätor*

Make dough and let rise as in recipe above. Shape and bake as Coffee Braids, p. 109.

Makes 2 braids.

Lucia Buns   *Lussekatter*

Early in the morning, about 5 or 6 o'clock on December 13th, Santa Lucia, the Queen of Light, comes into your bedroom. She is a young girl, a daughter, relative or friend of the family, dressed in white, bearing a lighted crown on her head, singing the Lucia song and offering coffee and traditionally-shaped Lucia buns.

Make dough for Saffron Bread, see recipe p. 110, and let rise. Roll out dough $3/_4''$ thick. Cut in 8" strips and shape into round strands. Shape into Lucia Buns, see color picture facing p. 113. Decorate with raisins. Place buns on greased baking sheets, cover and let rise until double in bulk (about 30 min.). Brush with beaten egg. Bake in very hot oven (450°F.) about 10 min. Cover and let cool on rack.

Makes $1^1/_2$–2 doz. buns.

Cardamom Coffee Cake   *Kardemummakaka*

$3^1/_4$ cup flour	*Topping:*
2 tsp. baking powder	2 tbsp. pearl sugar or
$1/_2$ cup butter	granulated sugar
1 cup sugar	$1/_2$ tbsp. cinnamon
2 tsp. crushed cardamom	$1/_3$ cup slivered almond
1 cup milk	

Sift together flour and baking powder. Cut in butter with pastry blender to pea-sized particles. Add sugar, cardamom and milk. Stir until well blended. Pour into greased 8" pan.

Sprinkle with cinnamon, sugar, and slivered almond.

Bake in moderate oven (375°F.) 50 min. Unmold. Serve slightly cooled.

CHRISTMAS GINGERBREAD HOUSE

CHRISTMAS BREADS AND COOKIES

From top to bottom: Christmas Stars; Ginger Snaps; Saffron Coffee Braid and Buns; Lucia Buns, various shapes such as Vicar's Hair, Christmas Wagons, Lucia Cats; Christmas Crullers; Almond Tarts; Jelly Cookies; Brandy Rings.

8

Danish Pastry *Wienerbröd*

Butter dough:
1/3 cup flour
1 1/2 cups butter
Yeast dough:
2 packages active dry yeast
1/4 cup water
1 cup cold milk
1 egg
1/4 cup sugar
3 1/2 cups flour

Filling:
apple sauce, Almond Paste
or Vanilla Cream

Sift flour for butter dough onto board. Cut in butter with pastry blender and toss together to a dough. Refrigerate.
Dissolve yeast in warm water (110°F.). Stir in cold milk, egg, and sugar. Add flour gradually, beating with wooden spoon until smooth and glossy. Turn dough onto floured baking board and knead until smooth. Roll out to 14" square. Spread butter dough evenly over half of yeast dough, leaving 2" border. Fold dough in half. Roll out fairly thin, fold in three parts. Refrigerate 10 min. Roll out. Repeat this three times. Cover and leave in refrigerator for 30 min. Roll out dough into 20" square and shape into envelopes, combs or crescents, see below. Place on ungreased cookie sheets. Let rise in room temperature, not too hot, about 1 hour. Brush envelopes and crescents with beaten egg. Bake in hot oven, 450°F., until golden brown, 10–15 min.

To shape envelopes: Cut dough into 4" squares. Spread center of each square with 1 teaspoon of each filling, see below. Fold corners toward center and pinch edges. Makes 25 pastries.

To shape combs: Cut dough in 5" strips. On each of the 4 strips place almond paste filling in the middle lengthwise and fold sides over. Cut each strip in 4" pieces and make 4 slashes about one third of way through the piece on one side. Let rise until double. Brush with water and dip combs in sugar and chopped almonds. Makes 20 pastries.

To shape crescents: Cut dough in 5" strips. Cut each of the 4 strips in triangles with 3" base. Place almond paste filling on base and roll up. Makes 28 pastries.

Almond Paste for filling: Mix 1/4 pound ground almonds with 1/2 cup sugar. Gradually add 1 egg and work until smooth.

114

Danish Pastry: Crescents, Envelopes, Combs · *Wienerbröd*

Vanilla Cream for filling: Mix in double boiler $1/2$ cup milk, 1 egg yolk, 1 tbsp. flour and 1 tbsp. sugar. Cook, stirring, until thick. Cool, stirring occasionally. Add $1/2$ tsp. vanilla.

Frosting: Mix $2/3$ cup powdered sugar with $1^1/2$ tbsp. water and stir until smooth and shiny. Spread over warm pastry before serving.

Filling
Shrove
Tuesday Buns

Fettisdags-
bullar or
Semlor

Shrove Tuesday Buns

Dough:

1 package active dry yeast
1/4 cup water
1/2 cup butter
1/2 cup milk
3 cups flour
1/4 cup sugar
1/4 tsp. salt

Fettisdagsbullar or *Semlor*

To brush:

1 egg white

Filling:

1/2 cup ground blanched
    almonds
1/2 tsp. almond extract
1 cup powdered sugar
1 egg white
1 cup whipping cream

Dissolve yeast in warm water (110°F.).
Melt butter in saucepan, add milk and let cool until lukewarm.
Mix 1 cup flour with all the other ingredients for dough. Beat with
wooden spoon until smooth, adding remaining flour gradually. Continue
beating until dough is smooth and firm. Cover and let rise in warm
place until double in bulk (about 1 hour). Punch down.
Turn dough onto floured baking board and work until smooth. Shape
into 12 buns. Place buns on greased cookie sheet, cover with towel and
let rise in warm place until double in size.
Brush buns with beaten egg white. Bake in hot oven (425°F.) until
golden brown, 10–12 min. Cool covered on rack.

Prepare almond paste for filling. Mix almonds, almond extract, sugar, and slightly beaten egg white. Work until smooth. If needed, add small amount of water.

Cut off top from buns, see picture. Fill with almond paste and garnish with whipped cream. Replace tops. Dust with powdered sugar.

Serve in deep individual dishes with hot milk, sugar and cinnamon. Makes 12 buns.

Swedish Puff Paste   *Smörbakelser*

1 cup cold butter	*Filling:*
1²/₃–2 cups pastry flour	jam or apple sauce or pitted
¹/₄ cup ice water	and finely chopped prunes

Sift flour onto baking board. Cut butter into flour with pastry blender. Gradually add ice water and shape to dough. Handle dough as little as possible. Chill for 30 min. or more. Roll out dough into a rectangle, about ¹/₄″ thick. Fold 2 times and roll out again. Chill. Repeat this procedure 3 times, chilling dough after each time.

Roll out dough 12″×12″. If difficult to handle, roll out between 2 sheets of wax paper.

Shape dough into Christmas Stars (see color picture, facing p. 113), Envelopes, or Butter Rings.

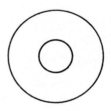

Christmas Star	*Envelope*	*Butter Ring*

For Christmas Stars and Envelopes, cut dough into 3″ squares. Fill 1 tsp. jam in center of each.

For Butter Rings, take out rings, 2″ across, brush with egg and spinkle with sugar and chopped almonds.

Bake in extremely hot oven (500°F.).

Remove cookies to racks and let cool uncovered.

Makes 16 Christmas Stars, or 16 Envelopes, or 36 Butter Rings.

117

Spicy Rye Rusks   *Kryddskorpor*

1 package active dry yeast	1/2 cup sugar
1/4 cup water	3/4 tsp. fennel seed, pounded
3/4–1 cup lard	3/4 tsp. anise seed, pounded
1 cup milk	1 1/3 cups rye flour
1/2 tsp. salt	3 cups all-purpose flour

Dissolve yeast in warm water (110°F.).

Melt fat, add milk and cool until lukewarm. Pour liquid into large bowl. Add salt, sugar, and seed. Stir in yeast and rye flour. Work with wooden spoon until smooth. Gradually, work in all purpose flour, saving about 3/4 cup of flour. Beat until smooth and firm. Sprinkle with flour, cover and let rise in warm place until double in bulk. Add about half of remaining flour and work until dough does not stick to bowl.

Turn dough onto floured baking board and knead well. Divide into 3 equal portions, shape into 3 loaves. Place on greased baking sheet. Let rise in warm place about 1 hour.

Bake in hot oven (425°F.) 20 min. or until golden brown. Remove to rack, cover and let cool.

Cut loaves lengthwise into 2 parts. Cut into 1″ slices.

Place on baking sheets and dry in very slow oven (200°F.) until dry and light brown. Turn off heat, keeping oven door slightly open, and leave rusks until thoroughly dry and crisp.

Makes about 100 rusks.

PLAIN CAKES

Sunday Cake   *Sockerkaka*

1/2 cup water	1 tbsp. grated lemon rind
1/4 cup butter	1 1/2 cups cake flour
3 eggs	2 tsp. baking powder
1 cup sugar, scant	

Bring water to the boiling point. Add butter and cool.

Beat eggs and sugar until light and fluffy. Add lemon rind.

Sift flour and baking powder together. Stir into egg mixture, gradually adding water. Do not stir batter too much. Pour into greased and breaded 9″ tube pan.

Bake in slow oven (325°F.) 35–45 min. Unmold and let cool, covered with towel.

Jelly Roll and
Chocolate
Roll

Rulltårta and
choklad-
rulltårta

Jelly Roll *Rulltårta*

3 eggs	1 tsp. baking powder
$1/2$ cup sugar	*Filling:*
$2/3$ cup flour	jam or apple sauce

Sift together flour and baking powder. Beat eggs and sugar until white and fluffy. Add flour mixture and stir until well blended. Pour into oblong pan lined with buttered aluminum foil.
Bake in hot oven (425°F.) 5 min. Turn onto wax paper sprinkled with sugar. Remove foil. Spread with jam or apple sauce. Roll up lengthwise. Wrap in wax paper.

Chocolate Roll *Chokladrulltårta*

3 eggs	*Filling:*
$3/4$ cup sugar	$1/2$ cup butter
$1/3$ cup cornstarch	$1/2$ cup powdered sugar
2 tbsp. cocoa	2 egg yolks
2 tsp. baking powder	1 tsp. vanilla

Beat eggs and sugar until white and fluffy. Sift together flour, cocoa and baking powder, and stir into egg mixture until well blended.
Pour batter into oblong pan lined with buttered aluminum foil. Bake in hot oven (425°F.) 5–8 min. Turn onto wax paper sprinkled with sugar and leave covered until cold, about 20 min.

Filling: Work butter and sugar until fluffy. Stir in egg yolks and vanilla. Spread cake with filling, roll up lengthwise. Wrap in wax paper.

119

Sand Cake   *Sandkaka*

1 cup butter, scant
3/4 cup cake flour
1 tbsp. baking powder
1 cup sugar

3/4 cup potato flour
3 eggs
2 tbsp. brandy
1 tsp. grated lemon rind

Melt butter and cool. Sift together cake flour and baking powder. Work butter, sugar and potato flour until white and fluffy. Add eggs and continue to beat. Add brandy, lemon rind and flour mixture. Stir until well blended.
Pour batter into buttered and breaded deep 9″ tube pan. Bake in slow oven (325°F.) 45–50 min. Unmold, cover, and let cool.

Ginger Cake   *Mjuk pepparkaka*

1/2 cup butter
1 cup sugar
3 eggs
2 tsp. cinnamon
2 tsp. ginger
1 1/2 tsp. cloves

1 3/4 cups flour
1 tsp. baking soda
2/3 cup sour cream
2 tbsp. lingonberry or cranberry
    preserve

Work butter and sugar until white and fluffy. Stir in eggs and spices. Add flour and baking soda sifted together alternately with cream. Stir until well blended. Pour into buttered 9″ tube pan. Bake in slow oven (350°F.) 50 min. or until cake does not stick to mold. Unmold, cover, and let cool.

Chocolate Cake   *Chokladkaka*

1/2 cup butter
2/3 cup sugar
2 eggs
2 tsp. vanilla

1/4 cup cocoa
1 tsp. baking powder
1 1/4 cups cake flour
1/2 cup light cream

Work butter and sugar until light and fluffy. Add eggs, one at a time. Add vanilla. Sift flour, cocoa and baking powder together and add alternately with cream. Pour batter into buttered and breaded 9″ tube pan. Bake in moderate oven (350°F.) 1 hour.

120

DECORATED CAKES AND TORTES

Sunday Cake with
Vanilla Cream Filling
Sockerkakstårta med vaniljkräm

See color picture, facing p. 49.

$1/3$ cup cake flour
$1/4$ cup cornstarch
1 tsp. baking powder
4 eggs, separated
$3/4$ cup sugar

Filling:
2 egg yolks
$1^1/_2$ tbsp. butter
1 tbsp. cornstarch
1 cup cream
2 tbsp. sugar
$1^1/_2$ tsp. vanilla extract
Icing:
1 cup powdered sugar
$1^1/_2$ tbsp. water
$1/2$ tbsp. lemon juice

Sift flour with cornstarch and baking powder. Beat egg whites until stiff. Add sugar, egg yolks and flour mixture. Stir carefully until well blended.

Pour into buttered and breaded round 9″ cake pan or frying pan. Bake in moderate oven (350°F.) 30 min.

Filling: Mix all ingredients except vanilla in double boiler and simmer until smooth and thick, stirring constantly. Remove from heat and beat occasionally until cold. Add vanilla.

Mix all ingredients for icing and stir until smooth.

When cold, cut cake into 2 or 3 layers. Spread filling between layers. Decorate with whipped cream or icing and candied fruit, see color picture, facing p. 49.

Mazarin Cake
Mazarintårta

$1/2$ cup butter
$1/4$ cup powdered sugar
1 egg yolk
$1^1/_4$ cups cake flour
Filling:
$1/2$ cup sugar
$1/3$ cup butter

$2/3$ cup ground blanched
almonds
2 eggs
5–6 drops green coloring,
optional
1 tsp. almond extract
1 tsp. sifted cake flour

Continued next page.

Work butter and sugar until white and fluffy. Add egg yolk and flour and stir until smooth. Leave dough in refrigerator 1 hour.

Filling: Work sugar and butter until smooth. Add almond, almond extract, eggs, green coloring, and flour, and mix until well blended.

Roll out dough between two sheets of lightly floured wax paper. Remove one sheet of wax paper and remove pastry to buttered 8″ pie pan. Remove the other paper sheet. Pat pastry firmly into pan. All air-bubbles should be removed. Spread filling over pastry. Bake in slow oven (325°F.) 45–50 min. or until filling is set. Cool in tin. Unmold carefully. Sprinkle with powdered sugar or cover with icing (1/2 cup powdered sugar mixed with 1 tbsp. water).

Mazarin Tarts   *Mazariner*

Proceed as above but place dough and filling in small individual tart shells. Bake in moderate oven (350°F.) 15 min. Top with icing or powdered sugar.
Makes 16 tarts.

Opera Torte   *Operatårta*

4 eggs	1 tbsp. cornstarch
2/3 cup sugar	1 cup milk
3 tbsp. cake flour	2 tsp. vanilla
3 tbsp. cornstarch	1 cup heavy cream
1/2 tsp. baking powder	*Almond Paste:*
Cream Filling:	1 cup blanched almonds
1 1/2 tsp. unflavored gelatin	2/3 cup powdered sugar
2 tbsp. cold water	1 1/2 tsp. almond extract
2 egg yolks	1 1/2 tbsp. egg white
3 tbsp. sugar	green food coloring

Mix 3 egg yolks with one egg, add sugar and beat until white and fluffy. Sift together flour, baking powder and cornstarch. Add to mixture. Beat remaining egg whites stiff; fold in carefully. Pour batter into 2 buttered and breaded round 8″ layer cake pans. Bake in moderate oven (350°F.) 12–15 min. Let cool.

Filling: Soak gelatin in small amount cold water. Mix egg yolks, sugar, cornstarch, and milk in double boiler and cook gently until smooth and thick, stirring constantly. Remove from heat, add gelatin and vanilla and beat occasionally until cold. Fold in whipped cream.

Ambrosia
Cake,
Uppåkra
Cookies,
Almond
Rusks, Rye
Cookies, and
Meringues

*Ambrosia-
kaka,
uppåkrakakor,
mandel-
skorpor,
rågkakor,
maränger*

Almond Paste: Put almonds through grinder twice. Work with sugar, egg white, almond extract and coloring 10 min. or until smooth. Roll out on wax paper; shape in large circle.

Divide each cake in two layers. Spread filling between layers and on top of cake. Cover cake with Almond Paste and sprinkle with powdered sugar. Keep in refrigerator until serving time.

Ambrosia Cake   *Ambrosiakaka*

2 eggs

$^2/_3$ cup sugar

2 tsp. grated orange rind

$^2/_3$ cup butter

$^2/_3$ cup cake flour

$^3/_4$ tsp. baking powder

Icing:

2 tbsp. orange juice

1 cup powdered sugar, sifted

3 tbsp. chopped candied orange peel or chopped almonds

Beat eggs and sugar until white and fluffy. Add orange rind. Work butter until creamy and add to egg mixture. Sift together flour and baking powder and stir in until well blended.

Pour into one buttered round layer pan $1^1/_2'' \times 8''$ and bake in slow oven (325°F.) about 30 min. Cool cake in pan 10 min. before unmolding. Let cool.

Icing: Stir sugar and orange juice until smooth. Spread evenly over cake and sprinkle with orange peel or finely chopped almonds. Makes 12 pieces.

Thosand
Leaves Torte

*Tusenblads-
tårta*

Thousand Leaves Torte   *Tusenbladstårta*

1 cup cold butter, unsalted
2 cups flour
¹/₄ cup ice water
Filling:
apple sauce
Vanilla Cream Filling
  (page 121)
Icing:
1¹/₂ cups powdered sugar, sifted

1 tbsp. water
1¹/₂ tbsp. lemon juice
Garnish:
¹/₂ cup heavy cream, whipped
  with 1 tsp. sugar
candied orange peels, cut
  in strips
slivered toasted almonds

Sift flour into bowl. Cut in butter with pastry blender. Gradually add
ice water and toss gently to a dough. Divide into 6 portions and shape
them into balls. Cover and refrigerate 30 min.

Roll out each ball very thin between sheets of wax paper or use pastry
cloth and cut out 8″ circle. Remove top sheet of paper. Prick cake
with fork. Place layers with wax paper underneath on cookie sheet.
Brush with ice water and sprinkle each cake with 1¹/₂ tbsp. sugar.

Bake in very hot oven (450°F.) 6–8 min. or until golden brown. Let
cool on wax paper.

Spread layers alternately with apple sauce and Vanilla Cream Filling.
Cover top with icing. Garnish with candied orange peels, almonds and
whipped cream forced through pastry tube.

Christmas
Ginger Snaps

Julpepparkakor

GINGER SNAPS

Christmas Ginger Snaps   *Julpepparkakor*

1/3 cup water
1/3 cup dark corn syrup
3/4 cup light brown sugar
1/2 cup butter
1 1/2 tsp. cinnamon

1 1/2 tsp. ginger
1 tsp. cloves
1 1/2 tsp. baking soda
4 cups flour

Bring water, syrup and sugar to the boiling point. Add butter and stir occasionally until butter is melted. Chill.

Add spices and baking soda mixed with small amount of flour. Gradually stir in flour until dough is very soft. Cover and refrigerate overnight.

Turn dough onto baking board and work until smooth.

Roll out dough thin, using pastry cloth, and cut out cookies with round or fancy cutters, see picture.

Place on greased cookie sheet and bake in hot oven (400°F.) 8–10 min. Let cool before removing to rack.

Decorate, if desired, with icing, (1/2 cup powdered sugar and 1/2 egg white beaten together until smooth) forced through fine paper tube, see picture.

Makes about 150 cookies.

125

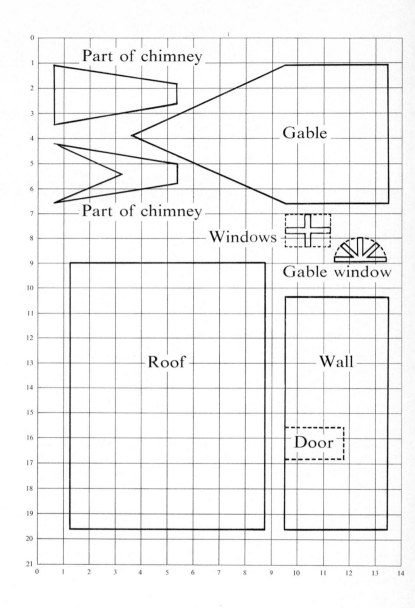

Part of chimney

Gable

Part of chimney

Windows

Gable window

Roof

Wall

Door

Pattern for Christmas Gingerbread House.
Cut out two pieces of all parts except windows of which ten are needed.

Christmas Gingerbread House   *Pepparkaksstuga*

3/4 cup heavy cream
1¼ cups brown sugar
2/3 cup dark syrup
1/2 tbsp. ginger
1/2 tbsp. grated lemon rind
1 tbsp. baking soda
4½ cups flour

Whip cream, add sugar, syrup, ginger, lemon rind, and baking soda and stir 10 min. Add flour and work until smooth. Cover and leave in refrigerator overnight.
Turn dough onto floured baking board and roll out about 1/8″ thick. Remove dough to greased baking sheet. Lay pattern on top and cut out, using sharp knife, see pattern opposite page.
Bake in moderate oven (350°F.) 10—15 min. Leave on sheet to cool. When cold, join pieces together by dipping edges in sugar melted in frying pan. Decorate with icing (1/2 cup confectioner's sugar and 1/2 egg white beaten together until smooth), forced through fine paper tube, and candy, see color picture, facing p. 112.

Almond Ginger Snaps   *Skurna pepparkakor*

1 cup butter
1 cup sugar
1/2 cup dark syrup
1 tbsp. ginger
2 tsp. cinnamon
2 tsp. cloves
1 tsp. baking soda
3½ cups flour
1 cup blanched almonds

Work butter until creamy. Add sugar, syrup, spices, baking soda, almonds and flour. Turn onto floured baking board and knead until smooth. Shape into 2 thick, slightly flattened rolls. Wrap each roll in wax paper and chill thoroughly.
Cut rolls with sharp knife into thin slices. Bake on greased baking sheet in very hot oven (450°F.) 8–10 min.
Makes about 150 ginger snaps.

COOKIES

Sweet Pastry

Mördeg

This is a basic dough used for many different cookies, flavored and shaped in different ways.

2¹/₂ cups flour
1 cup butter
¹/₂ cup sugar

Combine flour, butter and sugar on baking board and work together to a soft dough. Chill.

Coffee Fingers

Finska pinnar

Follow basic recipe for Sweet Pastry, above.

Topping:
1 egg white, slightly beaten

¹/₄ cup chopped almonds
3 tbsp. sugar

Divide dough into 6 parts. Roll each part by hand into round strands about the thickness of an index finger. Put strands close together. Brush with egg and sprinkle with mixture of almonds and sugar. Cut strands in 1¹/₂″ pieces, see picture. Place on buttered cookie sheet. Bake in moderate oven (350°F.) about 15 min. or until golden yellow.
Makes about 60 cookies.

Refrigerator Cookies

Brysselkex

Follow recipe for Sweet Pastry, above, and add 1¹/₂ tsp. vanilla. Do not chill dough. Shape dough into 2 rolls about 1¹/₂″ thick. Roll in sugar mixed with cocoa and wrap in wax paper. Chill. Cut rolls with sharp knife into ¹/₈″ thick slices. Place on buttered cookie sheet. Bake in moderate oven (350°F.) 6–8 min. Leave on sheet to cool.
Makes about 60 cookies.

Checkerboard Cookies

Schackrutor

See color picture, facing p. 49.

Follow recipe for Sweet Pastry above. Divide dough into 2 portions. Add 2 tbsp. cocoa to one portion and work until cocoa is evenly mixed

128

into dough. Add $1^1/_2$ tsp. vanilla to the second portion and work into dough.

Divide each portion into 2 pieces. Roll by hand into long strands about the thickness of an index finger.

Put the 4 round strands together checkerboard style. Press together tightly. Wrap dough in wax paper. Chill. Cut with sharp knife into $1/_4''$ thick slices. Place on buttered cookie sheets. Bake in moderate oven (350°F.) 8–10 min.

Makes 70 cookies.

Brandy Rings   *Konjakskransar*
See color picture, facing page 113.

Follow recipe for Sweet Pastry, p. 128, but add 2 tbsp. brandy to dough. Chill. Roll out on slightly floured baking board into thin round strands. Twist them 2 by 2 together and cut in 5'' pieces. Shape into rings, pinching ends together. Place on buttered baking sheets. Bake in moderate oven (350°F.) 6–8 min. or until golden yellow.

Makes about 55 cookies.

Sprits Cookies   *Spritsar*

Follow recipe for Sweet Pastry, p. 128, but add $1/_2$ egg and $1^1/_2$ tsp. vanilla to dough. Do not chill. Press dough through cookie press into long strips, placing strips parallel. Cut into 4'' pieces and shape, if desired, into rings or "S".

Place on buttered cookie sheet. Bake in moderate oven (350°F.) 8–10 min.

Makes 40–50 cookies.

Diagonals   *Spårkakor*

Follow recipe for Sweet Pastry, p. 128, but add $1/_2$ egg yolk to dough. Roll out $1/_3$ of dough into two strips about 2'' to $2^1/_2''$ wide. Place on buttered cookie sheet. Press remaining dough through cookie press, making three rows on each strip. Force currant jelly through small paper tube between rows.

Bake in moderate oven (350°F.) 10 min. When strips are cold, cut into 1'' diagonals.

Makes about 40 cookies.

Vanilla Rocks   *Vaniljkakor*
See color picture, facing p. 49.

Follow recipe for Sweet Pastry, p. 128, but add $1/2$ egg and 2 tsp.
vanilla to dough. Do not chill dough.
Force dough in tops through broad pastry tube onto buttered cookie
sheet. Bake in moderate oven (350°F.) 8–10 min. or until golden
yellow.
Let cool and garnish in center with jelly. Makes about 50 cookies.

Uppåkra Cookies   *Uppåkrakakor*
See color picture, facing p. 49.

Follow recipe for Sweet Pastry, p. 128, but use $3/4$ cup potato flour
and $1^1/2$ cups all-purpose flour. Add $1/2$ tsp. vanilla extract. Chill.

Garnish:
1 egg, slightly beaten
$1/3$ cup blanched chopped
   almonds
3 tbsp. sugar

Roll out thin on floured baking board using pastry cloth. Cut out round
cookies 2″ across. Fold each cookie, see picture, p. 123. Brush with
beaten egg and sprinkle with mixed sugar and chopped almond.
Place on buttered cookie sheet, bake in moderate oven (350°F.) 10
min. or until golden yellow. Makes about 55 cookies.

Jelly Cookies   *Syltkakor*
See color picture, facing p. 113.

Follow recipe for Sweet Pastry, p. 128, but add $1/2$ egg to dough. Chill.

Garnish: *Filling:*
1 egg, slightly beaten   jam or jelly
2 to 3 tbsp. sugar
$1/3$ cup chopped almonds

Roll out dough $1/8$″ thick, using pastry cloth. Cut out round cookies.
Cut out center from half number of cookies with a thimble. Brush with
egg white, and sprinkle with almond and sugar. Leave the other
cookies plain. Place cookies on buttered baking sheets. Bake in moderate oven (375°F.) 10 to 12 min. When cold, put together cookies,
2 by 2, one of each type with jam between. Makes about 40 cookies.

Almond Tarts
See color picture, facing p. 113.

Sandbakelser, Mandelformar

2/3 cup butter
1/3 cup sugar
1 egg yolk

1/2 cup blanched grated
almonds
11/2–13/4 cups flour

Work butter and sugar until creamy and flufffy. Add egg yolk, almond and flour and mix thoroughly. Chill. Coat inside of small fluted tins with dough, using floured thumbs.
Bake in moderate oven (350°F.) until light brown (about 10 min.).
Turn upside down on plain board. Allow to cool before removing tins.
Serve plain or filled with jam and whipped cream.
Makes about 35 tarts.

Almond Rusks

Mandelskorpor

1 egg
1/2 cup sugar
1/4 cup butter, melted
1/4 cup chopped almonds

1/2 tsp. almond extract
11/4 cups all purpose flour
1 tsp. baking powder

Beat eggs and sugar until white and fluffy. Add melted butter and almonds. Sift flour and baking powder together and stir into egg mixture until well blended. Roll dough with hands into 2 round strands about 11/2″ across. Place on buttered baking sheet. Bake in moderate oven (350°F.) 10 min.
Cut in 1/2″ slices. Separate slices and return to very slow oven (250°F.) 8 min. Turn off heat and leave in over to dry (about 20 min.). See picture, p. 123.

Oat Cookies

Havrekakor

1 cup all purpose flour
2 cups oatmeal

1 cup butter
1/2 cup sugar

Mix ingredients on baking board; knead until well blended. Roll dough into small balls and flatten crosswise with fork.
Place on buttered baking sheet and bake in moderate oven (375°F.) 8–10 min. or until light brown.
Makes about 50 cookies.

Christmas Crullers   *Klenäter*

Crullers are a typical Christmas delicacy, served with jam as dessert
or with coffee, see color picture, facing p. 113.

4 egg yolks	1$1/2$ cups flour
$1/2$ cup powdered sugar	*To fry:*
3 tbsp. butter	deep fat
1 tbsp. brandy	
1 tbsp. grated lemon rind	
$1/4$ tsp. salt	

Beat egg yolks, sugar and butter a few minutes. Stir in brandy, lemon
rind, salt and enough flour to make dough hold together but not more.
Chill dough.
Turn dough onto floured baking board. Roll out dough $1/16''$ thick. Cut
strips with pastry wheel $3/4''$ wide and $3''$ long. Cut gash in center and
twist end through, see picture, p. 133. Fry crullers in deep fat (375°F.)
until light brown. Drain on absorbent paper.
Makes 50 cookies.

Rosettes   *Sockerstruvor*

For making these crisp fried shells a special rosette iron is required.
They come in various shapes such as stars, butterflies, shells and
others. Rosette irons are available in certain department stores and
specialty shops. See picture, p. 133.

2 eggs	*To fry:*
1 egg yolk	deep fat
$2/3$ cup heavy cream	
$1/3$ cup sugar	
1 cup flour	

Beat eggs, egg yolk and cream together. Sift flour and sugar together.
Add to egg mixture. Stir until well blended. Let stand 2 hours. Put
rosette iron in cold fat to cover. Heat fat to 375°F., remove iron, drain
a few seconds on absorbent paper and dip into well stirred batter.
Hold coated iron over hot fat a moment before dipping in fat. Cook
until golden brown. Slip rosette carefully from iron and drain cookie
on absorbent paper. Heat iron again and repeat. Sprinkle rosettes
with sugar.
Makes 40 rosettes.

Christmas Crullers   *Klenäter*

Frying Rosettes in deep fat   *Struvor*

Rye Cookies   *Rågkakor*

1 cup butter	1¹/₄ cups rye flour
¹/₃ cup sugar	1¹/₄ cups all-purpose flour

Work butter and sugar until creamy and fluffy. Add flour and mix thoroughly. Chill.

Turn dough onto floured baking board; roll out thin. Prick surface with fork and cut rounds with floured cookie cutter, 2¹/₂″ across. Cut round holes in cookies, see picture, p. 123.

Place on buttered baking sheet and bake in moderate oven (350°F.) until golden yellow (about 10 min.).

Makes about 50 cookies.

Dream Cookies   *Drömmar*

1 cup butter	1 tsp. baking powder
³/₄ cup sugar	2 cups sifted flour
2 tsp. vanilla	¹/₃ cup blanched almonds

Brown butter in saucepan until golden brown. Chill slightly over cold water. Pour into large bowl, but leave the thick particles of butter in pan. Let stand until butter is firm. Add sugar and vanilla, and stir until light and fluffy.

Sift flour and baking powder together and stir gradually into butter mixture. Work dough until smooth. Roll out into small balls. Place on buttered baking sheet with half almond on top of each. Bake in slow oven (300°F.) until golden yellow (about 25–30 min.).

Makes about 70 cookies.

Walnut Meringues   *Valnötsmaränger*

4 egg whites
1¹/₂ cups powdered sugar
1 cup chopped walnuts

Mix egg whites and sugar in bowl. Bring water almost to the boiling point but do not allow to boil. Place bowl over hot water and beat mixture vigorously 20 min. Fold in walnuts carefully. Drop teaspoonfuls of mixture on greased baking sheet and bake in very slow oven (250°F.) until light yellow (about 30 min.).

Makes about 25 meringues.

134

Preparing Cream Puffs

Petits choux

Polynées

Polynéer

See color picture, facing p. 49.

¹/₂ cup butter	*Filling:*
1 tbsp. sugar	³/₄ cup ground almonds
¹/₂ egg yolk	¹/₂ cup powdered sugar
1 cup flour	1 egg
	1 tbsp. water

Work butter and sugar until creamy. Add egg yolk and flour, and work until smooth. Chill.

Filling: Mix almonds, sugar, egg and water and beat until smooth and fluffy.

Coat inside of small fluted tins with dough, using floured thumbs. Fill ³/₄ of tins with filling. Roll out remainder of dough, cut in strips and arrange crosswise on top. Pinch edges. Bake in moderate oven (375°F.) until golden yellow, about 20 min.

Makes 18–20 cookies.

Cream Puffs

Petits choux

1 cup water	4 small eggs
¹/₄ cup butter	1 tsp. baking powder
1 cup flour	

Continued next page.

Heat butter and water to the boiling point. Remove from heat and add flour, all at once, stirring constantly.

Return to heat, and cook stirring, until mixture separates from sides of pan. Remove from heat. Cool a few minutes. Add slightly beaten egg, one at a time, stirring vigorously. Stir for about 15–20 min.

Sprinkle baking powder over mixture and stir until well blended. Spoon tablespoonfuls of batter on buttered baking sheet, or use pastry bag and tube, see picture, p. 135. Bake in hot oven (400°F.) until firm and golden yellow, about 20 min. (If removed from oven too soon, cream puffs will fall.)

Let cool, slit tops and fill with whipped cream or ice cream. Serve immediately.

Makes 12 puffs.

Almond Rings   *Mandelkransar*

20 blanched almonds, chopped	$1/_2$ tsp. almond extract
1 cup butter	2 egg yolks
$1/_3$ cup sugar	$1^1/_3$ cups flour
$1/_3$ cup ground, blanched almonds	

Butter small, ring-shaped tins and sprinkle with chopped almonds. Work butter and sugar until creamy. Add egg yolks, ground almond, almond extract and sifted flour and mix thoroughly. Spread evenly in tins and bake in slow oven (325°F.) 20 min. Let cool in tins. Makes 18—20 rings.

Almond Wafers   *Flarn*

See color picture, facing p. 49.

$2/_3$ cup blanched almonds	1 tbsp. flour
$1/_2$ cup sugar	2 tbsp. milk
$1/_2$ cup butter	

Grind almonds and mix with other ingredients in skillet. Stir over low heat until butter melts.

Drop teaspoonfuls of mixture about 4″ apart on well greased and floured cookie sheet.

Bake in moderate oven (375°F.) until light brown, about 7 min. Let cool 1 min. before removing cookies with sharp, slender knife. Place over rolling pin to shape.

Makes 25 cookies.

Swedish Index

139

English Index

A

Almond Apple Cake, 83
Almond Dumplings, 32
Almond Rings, 136
Almond Rusks, 131
Almond Tarts, 131
Almond Toffee, 104
Almond Wafers, 136
Ambrosia Cake, 123
Anchovies au Gratin, Swedish, 20
Apple Cake, Almond, 83
Apple Cake with Vanilla Sauce, 85
Apple Dumplings, Baked, 84
Apples, Baked, Stuffed, 84

B

Baked Apples, Stuffed, 84
Baltic Herring, Fermented, How to Serve, 72
Beef, Boiled, with Horseradish Sauce, 36
Beef Rolls, Braised, 37
Beef Soup with Dumplings, Clear, 32
Beef Stew, Browned, 35
Beef Tongue with Mushroom Sauce, 38
Bird's Nest, 15
Blueberry Pudding, see Rhubarb Pudding, 82
Brandy Rings, 129
Brown Beans, Swedish Style, 78
Browned Potatoes, 76
Butter Rings, see Swedish Puff Paste, 117

C

Cabbage Rolls, Stuffed, 54
Cabbage Soup, Browned, 30
Calf's Liver, Braised Whole, 40
Caramel Custard, 91
Cardamom Coffee Cake, 111
Caviar Custard, Swedish, 22
Caviar Dip, Swedish, 17
Checkerboard Cookies, 128
Cheese Soufflé, 23
Chef's Marinated Herring, 14
Chicken, Fried, Swedish Style, 45
Chocolate Cake, 120
Chocolate Pudding, Orange, 93
Chocolate Roll, 119
Chocolate Toffee, 104
Christmas Stars, see Swedish Puff Paste, 117
Cinnamon Buns, 110
Cinnamon Ring, 109
Clabbered Milk, 83
Cod, Baked, see Baked Whitefish, 63
Codfish Pudding, 70
Coffee Braids, 109
Coffee Bread, 108
Coffee Fingers, 128
Cornucopias, 92

142

S

Saffron Braids, 111
Saffron Bread, 110
Sailor's Beef Casserole, 36
Salmon, Baked, see Baked
Whitefish, 63
Salmon, Dill-Cured, 73
Salmon, Poached, 60
Salmon Pudding, 69
Salmon, Smoked, Served
Swedish Style, 72
Salt Herring, Marinated, 14
Sand Cake, 120
Sardines, Baked Fresh, 22
Sardines, Fried Stuffed, 68
Sardines, Jellied, 18
Sardines, Marinated, 18
Sardines, Marinated, Fried, 69
Shrimp, Creamed, see Creamed
Lobster, 27
Shrove Tuesday Buns, 116
Side Pork, Fried, 50
Smelts, Baked Fresh, 22
Smelts, Fried Stuffed, 68
Smelts, Jellied, 18
Smelts, Marinated, 18
Smelts, Marinated, Fried, 69
Smörgåsbord Meatballs, 26
Spareribs, Roasted, 46
Sprits Cookies, 129
Steak with Onions, Swedish, 38
Strawberry Parfait, 91
Strawberry Pudding, see
Rhubarb Pudding, 82
Stuffed Eggs, 17
Summer Soup, 30
Sunday Cake, 118

Sunday Cake with Vanilla
Cream Filling, 121
Swedish Anchovies au Gratin,
20
Sweet Pastry, 128
Sweet-Sour Sauce for Fish, 62
Sweetbreads, Creamed, 43
Sweetbreads, Fried, 43

T

Thousand Leaves Torte, 124
Toffee, Almond, 104
Toffee, Chocolate, 104
Trout, Poached, see Poached
Salmon, 60

U

Uppåkra Cookies, 130

V

Vanilla Rocks, 130
Vanilla Sauce for Apple
Desserts, 86
Veal Birds, Braised, 41
Veal, Boiled, with Dill Sauce, 44
Veal Dumplings for Cabbage
Soup, 31

W

Waffles, Dessert, 88
Walnut Meringues, 134
White Sauce for Lutfish, 102
Whitefish, Baked, 63

Y

Yellow Pea Soup with Pork, 31

144